I0063242

BUDGETING

FOR BEGINNERS

Become a Master Planner and Manager of Your
Personal Finances

(Easy Ways You Can Learn How to Budget Your
Money)

Sylvia Lawson

Published by Alex Howard

Sylvia Lawson

All Rights Reserved

Budgeting for Beginners: Become a Master Planner and Manager of Your Personal Finances (Easy Ways You Can Learn How to Budget Your Money)

ISBN 978-1-77485-067-1

All rights reserved. No part of this guide may be reproduced in any form without permission in writing from the publisher except in the case of brief quotations embodied in critical articles or reviews.

Legal & Disclaimer

The information contained in this book is not designed to replace or take the place of any form of medicine or professional medical advice. The information in this book has been provided for educational and entertainment purposes only.

The information contained in this book has been compiled from sources deemed reliable, and it is accurate to the best of the Author's knowledge; however, the Author cannot guarantee its accuracy and validity and cannot be held liable for any errors or omissions. Changes are periodically made to this book. You must consult your doctor or get professional medical advice before using any of the suggested remedies, techniques, or information in this book.

Upon using the information contained in this book, you agree to hold harmless the Author from and against any damages, costs, and expenses, including any legal fees potentially resulting from the application of any of the information provided by this guide. This disclaimer applies to any damages or injury caused by the use and application, whether directly or indirectly, of any advice or information presented, whether for breach of contract, tort, negligence, personal injury, criminal intent, or under any other cause of action.

You agree to accept all risks of using the information presented inside this book. You need to consult a professional medical practitioner in order to ensure you are both able and healthy enough to participate in this program.

Table of Contents

Introduction

This book contains proven steps and strategies on how to take control of your finances, get out of debt and build your future prosperity. This is where you will learn about the tools you need to, not only solve money problems, but to prepare you for financial success for the rest of your life.

I know what it's like to need a budget. I used to live paycheck to paycheck, counting down the days to the end of the month, praying I could hold on. Praying that a bill wouldn't arrive out of nowhere and blow my meager finances to smithereens.

Fast forward to today. I've given up my 9 to 5 job and now pass my time living in different parts of the world. Sure, I still work, but on my own terms, and in my own time.

The best thing is that I never have to worry: how will I pay my bills? Will I have enough money at the end of the month? Will I ever escape my debt? I haven't worried about that in a long time.

This is what I want to pass on to you. Not my lifestyle (that's yours to choose), but the freedom to make your own choices – not have your choices made for you by how much money is left in the bank.

If living life free from financial worry appeals to you, follow the steps outlined in this book and you can join the ranks of the financially secure.

Now, I didn't say it would be easy. Personal finances are often a touchy subject. Nobody likes to be told how to spend his or her money. Or rather, not spend their money.

I won't do that. I won't tell you not to have your favorite coffee or to miss a trip with friends – all to save money. What I will do is give you the tools, techniques and information that will allow you to make decisions like that with a free heart, and never have to wonder if you're doing the right thing or not.

So let's get started. Keep reading and take the first step on your road to financial freedom.

Thanks once again for downloading this book, I hope you enjoy it!

Chapter 1: The Importance Of Money Budgeting

As we grow from children through the teenage years and into young adults we are taught many things, both from our parents and through school, but the one thing the vast majority of people are never taught is how to budget money. Unfortunately this is the one skill that everyone needs to know. Keeping a proper budget and tracking, what your money is doing is the best way to stay out of debt and build wealth.

Money is a powerful tool in life if we learn to make it work for us. Most people work for their money but once they have it, more often than not they do not keep track of it once it hits their checking account. Learning to budget your money is an important step in your financial health. Once you have written down your income and expenses, you will start to see where you money is going and some of it may surprise you. It will be the small expenses that add up the quickest. Spending five dollars on lunch every day, or that morning coffee you get on the way to work can add up to several hundred dollars a month. That is money that could be doing more good if used more wisely.

Let's put some math to that. If you spend 5 dollars for lunch a day during the work week that's $25 a week or $100 a month, give or take $5. Over the course of a year that's $1200 spent on lunches. If you start adding all the other small expenses that occur every month, before long you may find you have enough to pay off any debt you may have, but also start saving towards a healthy financial future.

In the quest of learning to budget money, writing everything down is a key factor. Start with your income from the last month (or an average of the last three months if your income fluctuates heavily from month to month) and write that down at the top of a piece of paper. Now you know how much money you have to spend through the month, you can start figuring up all your monthly expenses. This includes everything from your mortgage and utility payments, car payments, credit cards on down to the smallest expenditures. Write these down keeping them in specific categories, which we will come back to later in this book. Subtract your expenses from your income and see what's left.

This budget, based on your actuals, is your first budget because it shows you what your money has been doing every month. Now that you have a budget you can look at, it becomes much easier to not only SEE where the money is going but also take back CONTROL of where the money is going. And when that happens you can start to set goals, both short term and long term, for your money.

It will take some time to get your money budget dialed in. Most people say that if they stick with it they start to get a firm grasp on their budget and money situation in about 3 months. If you never learned to properly budget money the best way to get started is to just get started. If budgeting sounds like a nasty word to you, think again. It is not difficult, constricting, or boring. It doesn't take years to master and it will yield results. What kind of results you may ask? Well, here are just a few.

First and foremost, you will have more money. That's what everyone wants, right? Well, you won't have more money to spend, but eventually you will be able to spend that money on things that you never dreamed you could have. By budgeting, you are eliminating unnecessary spending and reducing spending overall. You give yourself a certain amount of money to spend in each category of your life so that you have more money left over to save and invest which will earn you even more money.

Budgeting reduces stress. At first, it might seem more stressful trying to stay within your spending requirements and not going over. Very soon after you will be so used to it and have no problems sticking with your budget. It will become easier and you will stop having to worry about how you will afford things. If you know you have your rent or mortgage covered because it's in your plan. The same goes with all your other expenses. Budgeting helps to reduce future stress by completing your goals. What happens when you have an unexpected expense that's not in your budget? Well, if you had a goal to save an emergency fund of 6 months of living expenses and you have been working towards completing that goal or have completed that goal, you should be able to cover it. Budgeting helps you afford your life even if you aren't making six or seven digits a year.

Chapter 2: The Value Of Supplementing Your Income

Pro tip: Always hold 2 jobs, one to finance your daily needs & one to make you wealthy.

This piece of advice is so simplistic yet so utterly landscape-changing. The surprising thing is that very few people adhere to it. It is one thing to have a steady paycheck coming in at the end of the month: you could say it is a good thing even. However, the fixed pay of a job disallows you from truly leading the kind of life you would love to, and makes it more difficult to have the compound effect truly work for you "on a large scale."

A person who earns $5,000 per month and who manages to save $2,500 a month because he or she has a supplemental income that allows for it will see far superior results than the person with the same income and can only save $1,500 because he or she has nothing on the side and bills need to be paid anyway.

What does the chapter title mean?

Well, this book is not calling on you to hold two jobs that both have a fixed paycheck. Far from it, even though that is not a bad idea at all.

What we mean is that you should aim to pair your regular day job with a source of income that allows for some financial flexibility, and a capacity to channel higher amounts toward your savings or investment fund. You could say a business of some sort. It is true that not all of us can successfully set up a business venture and succeed. However, it is also true that anybody can set up a profitable side gig of some sort, and add to their income.

Take the example of Joe, from Los Angeles:

Joe is 25 and recently started working as a teacher. Every evening after work, rather than go straight home, he works a side gig as a soccer coach for a girls' team close to his home. Joe also did some programming courses when he was younger and has since managed to put this education to good use, putting up a couple of mobile apps for sale every other month. He also has a few simplistic video game titles out. Every so often, the apps and video games bring in passive income in the form of royalties. His gig as a soccer coach allows him to be close to a sport he loves, and allows him to earn performance-based bonus amounts on top of the flat fee he receives. Combined, his side gig incomes outweigh his regular pay package. He also saves significantly while living just as comfortably as his peers do. His finances are healthy.

This abstract example gives you an idea of what this chapter means by telling you to get "two" jobs. Look for something you love, or something that can give you passive income. You could create a landing page for different products sold online, trade baseball cards, start a blog, or do anything else that has supplemental income potential. The final chapter of this book will illustrate multiple examples.

In the same line of thought, you need to pay yourself first. Let's learn more about that and how it relates to the compounding effect.

Chapter 3: Budgeting Fundamentals

Your budgeting plan should be simple. In the beginning, most people feel stressed when budgeting. The process of resisting urges and old habits can be exhausting. A complicated budgeting plan will only confuse you. This will add more challenges to your already stressful financial life. In this chapter, we will discuss the basic process of budgeting. We will elaborate on each part of the process on succeeding chapters.

Budgeting Fundamental #1: Start with a goal

You should always have financial goals. Some financial goals are obvious. Everyone around us saves for a house, the kids' college fund, or for retirement, so we should do the same. Aside from these default financial goals however, most people are confused with what they want to save for. We will discuss how you can arrive at a worthwhile financial goal later on. For now, you should think of the things or achievements that will make you genuinely happy. All your financial goals should lead to your happiness. It may also lead to the happiness of the people around you. If they do not, you will be working and sacrificing for nothing.

The planning stage

The next step is to develop a plan that will bring us closer to our goals. You can use the strategies in this book to start your budget planning. Most of the time, we already know what we need to do to be able to save money for our goals. However, because we do not put it in writing, we never get to apply our knowledge.

Planning organizes our ideas so that we can have a clear picture of what we need to do. Our plan should guide us in our daily financial decisions so that all our financial activities support the completion of our goals.

Time for Action

After planning, we need to make sure that we actually put our plan to action. The ideal scenario is that we will do exactly what is written on our plans. Old habits and urges to spend will challenge our abilities to put the plan in action. Your ability to resist them is crucial for the success of your plan.

Everything in moderation

Budgeting prevents us from spending too much on something. Our budget planning will only be successful if we do everything in moderation. Let's take drinking for example. Most adults drink. Most drinkers practice it in moderation. However, there are those who overdo drinking. The constant visits to the pub make them spend more on alcoholic beverages than the average person does. Because of drinking's many biological effects, the alcoholic's productivity and overall self-control are also affected. The disturbance in his productivity may affect his income while his lack of self-control when he is drunk may lead to more unnecessary expenses. The same pattern happens with all addictive habits.

When budgeting, your aim is to keep your spending in each aspect of life in moderation. You need to become accustomed to regular priced items rather than their expensive counterparts. If you really want to be efficient in the ways you spend your money, you should also avoid expensive brands. Buying expensive brands is only acceptable if they provide exceptional quality and if they will last longer than their less expensive counterparts.

100% Awareness

We can only practice moderation in all aspects of life if we are constantly aware of how we use our money. You need to know how much money you have in all your accounts at all times. In the chapters that follow, we will discuss the multiple tools that you can use to be constantly aware of your finances. By being aware of your spending, you will know if you are following the budgeting plan or if you are deviating from it.

This is where most people fail when budgeting. They make a great budget plan and they try to implement it. At the beginning of the process, their awareness of their expenses is at its peak. After a while however, they become bored of the plan. They begin to become less interested in their expenses. Their awareness level begins to go down. When this happens, the budgeter may fail to take note of some expenses. This will lead to some inefficient spending practices. The accumulation of bad spending practices will decrease the likelihood that the goal will be reached.

As soon as you start implementing your budget plan, you need to make sure that you have 100% awareness of your spending habits. We will discuss how you can achieve this in future chapters.

Performance analysis and budgeting remedies

You need to analyze your expense records to see if you are getting closer to your goals. You will not be able to implement your plan to perfection on your first try. In the beginning, habits developed in the past will severely affect your performance. If you have 100% awareness of your spending activities, you will be able to identify which habits cause the most financial damage.

When you identify these problem areas, the next step is to find remedies that will stop the financial bleeding. You should then insert these remedies to your plan as you revise it.

Chapter 4: What Is A Budget And Why Do I Need One?

A budget is simply a useful way for you to look at your money. It allows you to see how much is coming in, and if you do it honestly, how much is going out. In simplest terms, it is a document which compares your income to your outgo (expenses versus spending).

Keeping a monthly budget lets you visualize your financial situation - good, bad, or in-between. That visualization, or snapshot, if you will, is what gives you control over your money, instead of your money, or lack of it, controlling you. Later, we'll talk about how to use a budget to accomplish your financial goals, such as sending your child to college, buying a new home, or even just taking a much needed vacation.

Though it is a simple thing, a budget is also powerful tool. For instance, it can tell you where your cash is going each month. How many times have you looked in your wallet, expecting to see the $40.00 you just put in there, only to find receipts instead? Or worse, nothing at all? If you keep track of your cash spending in your budget by actual expense, like "Starbuck's" or "dining out", not by overall category, like "cash", you will soon be able to see the trends in your spending. And once you have done that, you can decide where to cut back each month to save money, like on your dinners out. You can also cut back, or even cut out, your Starbuck's spending. You'd be amazed how much you'll save, and how quickly.

A budget can also help you to plan for future expenses. Let's say your power bill fluctuates all year. A quick review of the past year's bills (or budgets if you've been doing it that long) will give you the ballpark figures you need to plan for any given month of the year.

How does the budget help you? It lets you see where you may have extra money to pay an upcoming power bill if you've guestimated it to be larger than the last. Or, better yet, it can show you areas where you can start saving months in advance for the higher power bills.

For instance, if your power bill runs around $120 in the fall, but you've budgeted $150 during the summer months, instead of spending the difference when fall rolls around, save that $30 a month for when the power bill goes up to $145 in the winter months. You can also save by "trimming the fat", like the Starbuck's expenses and dining out.

A budget can also help you plan for emergencies, cover unexpected bills when they pop up, and help you save for retirement. So let's get started!

Getting Started

First things first. Decide how you want to do your budgets. Do you want to write them out in a notebook? Do you want to use one of the free spreadsheets and/or free budgeting software available on the web? Or, do you want buy a higher end software? Do you want to use a spreadsheet or a program? You may have to play with these a bit to decide what is best and most comfortable for you. Doing your monthly budget should be easy, not vexing or something that you dread.

For instance, "dsBudget" is a free budgeting software available for download through CNET. It has 4 out of 5 stars from users. The description is almost exactly what we talked about in the last section. It may be a good program to look at if you want to go that way. You can always uninstall it if you don't like it.

If you have Microsoft Office, the spreadsheet, Excel, is a great tool. If you don't have Microsoft Office, "Open Office", a free suite of programs, also has a spreadsheet.

Mint, from Intuit, is an all-in-one tool that taps into all of your financial accounts and bills to give you the clearest picture of where your money is traveling. It has built in categories so you can keep up with your budget easily. It's great for people who like all that busyness because it is intuitive and really does so much of the work for you. But, some people don't like graphs and charts and just want to know the bottom line. They may not like Mint. It is, however, one of the most popular and highest rated programs on the web. It got a 5 out of 5 from PC Magazine and is first on lifehacker's "Five Best Personal Finance Tools" list for 2014. Best of all, it's FREE.

"You Need a Budget" – YNAB – does essentially the same sorts of things as Mint, bringing all of your income and outgo together for you to see on one screen. But, what the majority of users like the most seems to be the educational materials within the software that help you with your budget, as well as the videos, tutorials, and user community. And, it scored a ten on ease of use on 10TopTenReviews as well as being one of PC's picks and lifehacker's number two pick. True, the software costs $60, but it is frequently on sale, not only through its own website, but also on steam. You can get a month free (34 days) to try it out as well.

There are dozens of other good programs out there. Some are free; some are not. Some, like YNAB and AceMoney ($34.99) provide learning tools to help you create your budget and meet your financial goals. Ace Money is 10TopTenReviews number one pick for 2015. Some of the other programs ranked highest by lifehacker, PC, and 10TopTenReviews for 2015 are, GnuCash (free), Quicken Starter Edition,($114.99) and Office Time,($47) which is really geared toward small business owners, freelancer, and self-employed persons in general. It helps you track your time and create invoices, among other things. PC gave it a 4.5 out of 5.

Once you have decided on the form you will use, gather all of your bills together in one stack. We know that you may well have other expenses like child support, or daycare. Make a note for all expenses for which you have no bills and mark the amount of the obligation and the date due. Then gather all of your paystubs, commission checks, investment returns or other evidence of income in a separate stack.

We realize that some of these items of income do not come in monthly. If you have your past year's income from that source to compare it to, add any increase you have gotten this year, then divide by twelve and you'll have your number for the monthly budget. However, if you get paid a quarterly dividend, for example, and you are more comfortable entering the income in the month it is received, that's entirely up to you. This is your budget, your tool.

Chapter 5: Tips For Budgeting

If you are a beginner to budgeting, then the pointers suggested in this chapter will definitely help you out. These pointers will not only helping you to formulating a budget but also sticking to it. I have also listed out some budgeting tools that can assist you with this.

Budgeting tips:

One of the important aspects of budgeting is reducing your expenses. Half the time, we tend to cross our budgets because we end up spending more than we anticipated. Hence, I have mentioned some pointers pertaining to the reduction of expenses in this chapter.

Learn to be flexible

It is certain that we will not be able to follow our budget exactly. This is because; sometimes our expenses may be more than what we expected. Hence the key is to have a liberal mindset when you formulate your budget. This way, you will be in a safe place even when met with the worst-case scenario. On the contrary, if you have a conservative budget, you tend to become flustered if your expenses exceed the budget. So try and leave a little money as an emergency fund for your monthly expenses. This amount should be utilized only for your emergency expenses and not be used for anything else. Don't go to this money if you are trying to buy something over and above your monthly needs and after fulfilling your monthly luxury needs. This is for those times that you really have to make an urgent purchase such as a laptop because your old one suddenly went kaput. So be prepared for any type of emergency and remain flexible with your budget.

Make room for some fun

All work and no fun make every day dull. Similarly, a budget that does not take into consideration the expenses you might have to incur in connection with having fun is a boring one. When you don't make room for your leisure activities in your budget, you will feel frustrated after spending money on such activities. A conservative budget is not going to stop us from having fun. We might as well plan for these expenses instead of regretting after spending. Moreover, when we set aside a sum every month for fun activities, we will be able to have fun in an organized fashion. You will see in the sample budget that entries such as "leisure time" and "club" money have been added in. these are important for everyone. You cannot stop socializing just because you have to stick to a budget. You need to entertain yourself in order to function properly. There are many people who will not add these charges to their budget thinking it will get adjusted. But nothing will get adjusted unless you consciously adjust it. So these charges are mandatory to be added into your monthly budget.

Spend below your income

Never spend more than what you earn. We tend to borrow and spend sometimes. Repayments of these debts become a problem next. This has to be borne in mind if you use a credit card to purchase things. Never exhaust the limit and buy more. This will increase the rate of interest associated with the card as well. Hence never spend over and above your income. If you have that kind of problem, then start taking a friend along so that they can stop you from making unnecessary purchases. You need to take with you your prepared budget everywhere you go so that you know how much you need to spend on something and where you need to curb your spending. If you think you are on the verge of over spending then consciously stop yourself and say to yourself, I will buy this next month.

Borrow for the right reasons

Borrow only if it is used to finance a long-term investment. This way, your asset will help you in repaying the debt incurred. For instance, if you take an education loan, you will be able to repay the loan from the income you earn because of your qualification. Similarly, if you invest in a house, you will be able to repay the loan from the rental income you are earning. Avoid borrowing for reasons that will not benefit you with the passage of time. For instance, you borrow money to buy a car. The value of the car depreciates over time and such an investment is not profitable if you are making it in the first place with a loan. Similarly, you decide to borrow to go on a lavish holiday. Once you are done with it, you are left with a big headache to pay the loan on time. So choose not to borrow for something that won't pay big over time and you are sure of having a good chance at making the money and paying off the debt duly.

Rent

Never wait till the first of every month to pay your rent. If you do have enough money before the beginning of the next month, pay off your rent instead of waiting for the first. You should do this without fail if you have any apprehensions of spending the money before the first of the upcoming month. Defaulting in the payment of your rent is something that you can easily avoid. If you do default then you will be troubles of all sorts. You will have to live with bad credit and might also get kicked out. These are problems you don't need especially if you are just starting out with your career.

Overpay your mortgage

It is not necessary that you have to pay only the stipulated amount towards your mortgage every month. If during any month, you have extra money, pay more than what is required for the mortgage. This way, you will be able to close it sooner and reduce the interest component. So choose to pay at least 10% more than you usually would in a month towards your mortgage. You can choose a bigger number as well if you think it will be easier for you to pay off your mortgage by contributing 15% extra than normal towards it. You need to come up with a good plan in order to do this.

Utilities

Invest in power saving utilities such as fluorescent bulbs. These reduce your electricity bill to a greater extent. Adjust the temperature of the thermostat to reduce your cooling and heating costs. Usage of ceiling fans will also help in reducing your electricity bill. These utilities are a onetime investment that can save a lot of expenses in the future. Hence apportion a part of your budget to take care of these expenses.

Transportation expenses

Plan to finish multiple errands in a single trip. This way, you can reduce the fuel consumption and thereby reduce the money spent on gas. This is also an effective way to manage your time.

Budgeting utilities:

Use one of the following systems to keep a tab on your money and follow your budget:

Notebook and pen

As simple as this may seem, sometimes all you need is a notebook and a pen to write down all your incomes and expenses. You can also maintain a separate column for the savings you make. Though these are least expensive ways of keeping track of your money, the risk of misplacing the notebook is always there. When you decide to sit down and prepare your budget just make sure that you have these handy and are not simply sitting down being unprepared for it or scamper at the last minute to find these.

Spreadsheet

Your simple looking excel can work wonders. This also helps in avoiding manual errors and you will be able to perform even complex calculations in a matter of seconds and get the most accurate figure. The best thing about using the spreadsheet is that once you set the formula for certain fields, you don't have to rework the entire thing even if you change the figures. So start by making a conclusive excel sheet for your budget and use it on a monthly basis to simply change the values in it. You can save a copy of it on all your devices and also mail it to yourself. The final goal is to have it ready on a monthly basis in order to quickly fill in the details and prepare the budget with ease.

Financial Software

There are several financial softwares available out there such as Microsoft money and Quicken. These are a complex version of your spreadsheet and are capable of tracking your income and expenses in a better way. This helps you to keep a tab on your investment accounts and bank accounts as well. You will have a chance to look all your accounts and know how much money you have and where. However, this is risky if someone else gains access to your computer. They will be able to access details of your finances in a jiffy.

Online Software

These days, you have different versions of online software that help you track your money and monitor your budget. Most of these are free while the others come at a minimal cost. As they are web based, you will be able to access the figures from anywhere. You will be able to update your expenses immediately without any delay. You can directly link all your bank accounts and have them unified. You will have a chance at tracking your expenses and won't have to roam around with a pen and paper. You will have everything at your fingertips and can easily make modifications to anything and everything that is related to your budget and finances. However, not many people would be comfortable in updating their financial information online. There is the threat of fraud and also identity theft. So remain wary of such dubious websites and choose something that is completely trustworthy and has a good reputation so that your money and identity are safeguarded. You can ask any of your friends for a suggestion to be safe.

Chapter 6: The Benefits Of Budgeting

Having Control

One of the benefits of having a budget is that you can exactly monitor how much money you spend each month or week. Knowing this, you can have greater control over your finances and you can easily check if there are issues that need to be addressed.

Also, having a budget will make it easier to adapt your finances to any changes due to unforeseen circumstances. If there are emergencies or unexpected increase in monthly bills, you will not panic because you are prepared for these kinds of situations.

Budgeting gives you the power over your money instead of letting your money drive you. It also allows you to plan whatever you want to do with it. Having control helps you decide whether to save your money, invest or use to eliminate debt.

Budgeting will change your mindset towards money and will help you develop the right behavior when using it. Instead of spending your money carelessly, you will be able to use it as a tool to fulfill your needs and reach your financial goals. You will learn how to control and discipline yourself to be more responsible in financial matters.

Clear Monitor

Another advantage of budgeting is that you will be able to know where your money is going. A budget is a valuable self-education tool that will show you how much money you earn, where it goes, and how much of it is left after you pay all your expenses. Budget can keep you from being surprised when you notice that your amount of your money is decreasing. Being able to monitor your expenses will help you have better plans in the future and encourages you to prepare for emergencies.

A detailed budget will help you monitor your improper ways in spending money. It can also help you identify the source of wastes so you can take action to correct them.

With budgeting, you will no longer wonder every month about where you spent your money. It also allows you to know what you can afford based on your financial status. It gives you a clear picture of your priorities based on how you spend your money and how it works for you. It also helps you have a longer-term view of your finances. By maintaining a good budget, you can prevent having a debt.

Having a financial monitor helps in ensuring that the amount of money that is going out is less than the amount coming in. Without this, you may spend money more than you have which can lead you getting into debt. It's easy to lose control of your finances when you are not keeping a budget plan because you cannot monitor the money that comes and goes.

Opportunities

When you don't have a strict budget, you often don't have enough money left for other opportunities such as saving for a car, buying a house, or starting a business. Budgeting allows you to save money for other purposes such as vacation, gifts, or celebrations.

By having a budget plan, goals can be set and reached such as building a house, raising up a business and funding college education for each child. Because budgeting encourages saving money, you will have enough finances to fulfill these goals.

Good Organization

Through budgeting, you can become more organized because it allows you to develop your skills in managing your personal finances, incomes, savings, and expenses. If expenditures exceed your earnings, you can make some corrections in the coming weeks or months to control the flow of your finances.

Creating a strict budget will lead the family to spend within the monthly income. The family will be more aware of the limits and will be more careful not to spend excessively.

By dividing your money into categories such as savings and expenses, a budget makes you more aware how each category takes portions of your money. A budget will also serve as a tool for organizing your financial statements and bills. By organizing all your financial transactions, you can surely save time and effort.

Better Communication

Money matters and financial issues are one of the most common reasons for arguments between couples. Most often, misunderstandings occur because of lack of planning and organization about financial matters. A budget plan can help you have a better communication with your spouse or family members. It allows you to communicate your ideas and discuss about the plan of how to use the money with your family members.

A family budget can help you share your goals, your financial issues, and your plans with other members. Family discussions about the budget can also help you know about the different priorities of each member that will enable you to address them well.

This will also promote teamwork with your family and prevents conflicts on discussions about how money is used. Budgeting will also teach each family member to be more responsible and accountable in spending money. It will develop understanding within the family and as well as unity.

Reduce worries

Following a budget allows you to prepare for the future emergencies. Having a monitor of your finances will help you see the potential financial problems that might happen along the way. You will be able to make changes before these problems occur.

By having a budget, you will also know how much debt load you can take without being worried about having not enough. You can even avoid having a debt once you have learned and maintained effective budgeting.

Savings

A budget plan provides many ways to save money of the monthly income for various purposes. Budgeting can help you manage your money and save more for short-term and long-term goals. Since you are more careful with your finances, you will learn to put savings at your highest priority.

In addition, budgeting allows you to prepare and set aside money for emergency purposes. When an unexpected demand comes, you can use your emergency savings. You will also learn how to manage your bills and eliminate unnecessary expenses like interests, fees, and penalties.

Budgeting clearly teaches you how to allocate your money according to your financial limitations. It saves you from overspending and sinking in debt. When you prioritize savings, you will be able to minimize your spending habits and learn to manage your money very well.

Chapter 7: Investing

It is the dream of many people to make some money and continue growing it but only a few people dare to invest. The truth of the matter is that the rich people in the society have all invested their money. The problem many people face is that they do not know how to invest from the ground going up. It will benefit you to learn what investing is all about and how you can go about in order to achieve your desired goals.

Investing basically means putting you money to work for you. This will always maximize your income even when you lose your job. There are so many ways one can invest their money these days, for instance:

In stocks: when you buy stocks or shares for a certain business, you become part owner of that business. You are entitled to business profits in terms of dividends and you are allowed to vote at the shareholder's meetings.

In bonds: bonds are securities that have been founded on debts. When you buy a bond, you are basically lending your money to a business or the government. In return, you get some interests and at the end of it all, you will get your money back.

In mutual funds: when you buy a mutual fund, you are contributing some money together with other investors, then you pay a professional manager who will be buying securities for you.

In real estate: this involves buying real estate properties and selling them at a profit.

Starting your own business: you can be an entrepreneur as well, where you invest your money in something that you really enjoy doing and earning more from it.

It is important to know more ways of investing so that you will have a variety of ideas to choose from. What potential investors need to know is that all these ways have their positive side and the negative side. You have to weigh both the advantages and the disadvantages keenly in order to choose how you will want to invest your money.

Why is Investing important?

People invest for different reasons, there are those that will invest in order to increase their personal freedom. If you are not investing, you might have to work for long hours every day in order to make a large amount of but if you are investing, you might have some free time to yourself and for the people that matter in your life.

Investing gives one a sense of security. You are assured that even if you lose your main source of income, you will have some money coming through from your investments.

Investing helps you afford more of what you want. There are so many people who only cater for their needs and that's that.

You will have to work harder in order to afford something extra. Investing can help you earn more in order to afford more at the end of the month.

Investing is a necessity in today's world. Things are not as easy as they were a few years back. You have to maximize your income in order to enjoy a good retirement and investing is a sure way to make some money for the future.

Investment Mistakes You Should Avoid

Making mistakes is common when one is investing but it always helps when you know some of the common mistakes so that you will be able to avoid them.

Investing with no plan: an investment plan will never fail you. You need to plan for your money and the goals that you want to achieve with the investment in order to give the investment some meaning. A plan will help you avoid losing money.

Do not invest when in debt. It is a rule of investors to clear off all their debts first before they can start setting some money aside for investment. It is always good to start at a clear slate, where you are in zero debts.

Having high expectations on returns on any investment is a mistake. Many people do not sit back to think of how the returns will come by and they end up investing money and immediately expecting so much more. When the returns are not as expected, you end up becoming frustrated. First of all avoid investment ideas that seem too good to be true. Take time to study an investment avenue and always have realistic expectations.

Investing following market conditions as these will keep changing all the time. There is not a single time that the market conditions will be the same for a long time. If you want to invest, the current market condition should never be a determining factor as it will mislead you and you might come to regret your decision later.

Chapter 8: When You Feel Like Life Is Nothing But Bills

Life is expensive. We live in a day and an age where everything costs money. Before long, you feel like all you do is spend money. After you're done spending it, you realize that you really don't have enough of it. It's a vicious cycle. How do we get around the fact that we have to pay to practically breathe? Finding a way to do what we like and need to do and still feel comfortable in our lives can be difficult.

Unfortunately, money has controlled our society for centuries. If you don't have it, you're poor, and if you have too much, then you're rich. There seems to be no middle ground to having the money that you need to survive. Then we look at the prices of everything rise while we don't make any more than we have made.

There has to be some way to combat the system so that we can live comfortably.

When bills seem to control our lives, we really aren't living. We are focusing on money and making payments. Think about it. We were meant to live for so much more than living from paycheck to paycheck.

The good news is, there are ways to do so. It may not be easy to get to the point where we can experience that financial freedom, but there are ways to get to it. In this book, I'm going to give you some tips and suggestions on how you can make enough to live a comfortable lifestyle and not feel as though you live paycheck to paycheck. Many of these are lifestyle changes, so you must be prepared to change aspects of your life in order to achieve you end goal.

So, if you're ready to find a way to enter into financial freedom, let's take a look at some methods that you can use to minimize your spending in order to gain extra monetary freedom!

Chapter 9: Types Of Personal Budgets

Line Item budgeting

Many of us make these kinds of budgets. In this case, you have a spreadsheet where you record each line item with an estimated cost. When you incur the expense, you then record the actual amount you incurred.

Percentage budget

In this case, you allocate percentages to the different expenditure categories. An example would be 50% for needs, 30% for wants and 20% for savings. You can also decide to pick another approach that would include the other mentioned expenses like housing and other major purchases

Cash budget

This is another easy way of budgeting for your needs. In this type of budget, each expense is allocated a specific amount of cash. It is however involving because recording should be done according to all expenditure involved.

Capital budget

This is commonly used in the corporate world where companies budget for the different capital expenses that they intend to incur. In our household setting, you can use it for the major purchases like the electronics, furniture and the rest of the items that are not replaced under a year.

Event budget

There are many times in the year that you are expected to hold a specific event or even attend one. Unfortunately, in both the occasions, it does come with the expectation of you spending. This is where an event budget comes in handy. You can be able to set aside funds that will be used in case of any upcoming event.

Category Budget

This works in a similar manner to the event budget. Some categories may just seem difficult to manage. You can classify them into categories and save money under each of the category.

Many of the budgeting techniques above seem pretty easy to follow but implementing is the hard part. To make it possible to implement all the above, you should use the envelop system, which we will discuss next:

Envelope system

This is best or most effective if you use cash. If you've been working on budgets like excel and different budgeting software but you still find yourself overspending, this is a good one for you. The reason for this is simple; nothing holds you accountable from overspending so all you do is pick money from whatever source and spend it. So as long as the money is there, you will spend it! With envelop budgeting, you put money in different envelops that you've labeled depending on the different areas of your spending. For instance, you could have envelops for rent, groceries, clothes, transport, etc. Whatever it is that you spend money on, should fit it in one of the categories. This means that you will need to have tracked your spending on the different item categories just to know how much money they usually cost if you don't want to end up with no money and being forced to overspend.

Ensure not to leave any money unassigned since this will probably be the money you will go for if you haven't planned for it. If you want to incur any expenditure, pick money from the most relevant envelop for that expense. So if you want to spend money on transport, pick the money from the transport envelop. Although it has a learning curve, you will definitely learn more of it as you go on. If you have no money in any of the envelops, then you cannot spend more money. Don't pick it from another category, especially if this is something you can live without. When you follow this system, it will be easier to know where you usually overspend.

In this chapter, we mentioned the budgeting process when discussing the types of budgets briefly. In the next chapter, we will go into detail on how to actually create a budget that works.

Chapter 10: Tactics

Goals are what you hope to achieve – tactics are how you get there. These are roughly in order from easiest to most complex, so once things start to sound too complicated or just uninteresting, you can just go ahead and skip to the next chapter. The good news is that the easy ones are very, very easy and employing them will make a big difference.

401k

You might know that a 401k has advantages when it comes to taxes – this is why people typically recommend investing in one. I agree that the tax benefits are good, but the most important thing about enrolling in a 401k plan is the fact that the money gets automatically deducted from your paycheck. The easiest way to save is to never have the money in the first place, and if you set up your 401k and forget about it, you'll suddenly look at it one day and find thousands of dollars that you never even considered spending elsewhere.

Another benefit of a 401k that many companies offer is matching. It's a simple concept – for every dollar you put in, they'll put in another dollar. You should absolutely, unequivocally always take advantage of any 401k matching. It's free money. There's a limit, usually as a percentage of your salary (so an employer will match up to 4% of your salary that you put into your 401k), so make sure you hit the limit. If your employer matches 4% and you put that much in, you're getting the equivalent of a 4% raise for doing nothing but saving.

When signing up for a 401k, you may be asked to pick where your money is invested – a 401k is just a type of account, but the money still needs to be invested in something (usually stocks). By default, you'll generally be in a target date retirement plan – the name will be something like "2055 Retirement Target

Date Plan." This just means that someone else will manage the money invested there under the assumption that you're going to retire around 2055. If you don't want to bother learning about the different plans available to you, then just leave it in the default one. If you want to spend a little more effort, I recommend moving your money into an S&P index fund if one's available (more on that below).

S&P ETF

You're putting some money in your 401k, but because you're a responsible saver, you have other money left over too. What do you do with it?

This is one of the key questions to financial planning, and it's one of the ones that can be the most overwhelming to think about. The good news is that if you don't want to think about it, there's an easy answer — exchange traded funds (ETFs).

An ETF is basically a bunch of stocks that somebody else selects based on some particular criteria. There are thousands of them, but what you want is an S&P ETF. The S&P is just a measure that tracks the whole stock market by following 500 of the most important stocks, and an S&P ETF is one that buys those same 500 stocks. The reason that's what you want to buy is because it means you don't have to think about which stocks are going to do well and which aren't – on average, the market as a whole goes up year after year, and if you're in an S&P ETF, so will your money.

So how do you actually go about putting your money into an ETF? First, you'll need a broker – this is just a company that buys and tracks your stocks for you. A brokerage account is basically a bank account but with stocks in it instead of cash.

One of the best brokerages these days is **Robin Hood**. It's a free app that lets you buy and sell stock with absolutely no fees (most brokerages charge you some money each time you buy or sell). All you have to do is download the app and follow their instructions, transfer some money in, and you're ready to go. From there, you really just need to search for stock symbol SPY – this is one of the best S&P ETFs. If you just put all of your extra money into that and don't think any further about your investments, you'll do perfectly well.

Automated investing platforms

There's one category of companies that's providing a very valuable alternative to opening your own brokerage account and buying ETFs. These are automated investing platforms like Betterment and Wealthfront, and they're designed to make it as easy as possible to invest for your future.

The premise is simple – you deposit your money in an account with one of the services, and they ask you questions about your current financial situation and your plans for the future. Based on that, they automatically invest your money. The investments are all good, simple ones (many of them are ETFs). When you're young, they pick investments that are a bit riskier (unless you tell them not to), since those tend to grow faster, and as you get older they shift your investments into things that are more conservative.

If you want to invest in the absolute easiest way possible and not think at all about what your money is invested in, I highly recommend these services. They're truly as simple as it gets, but they'll do the right things with your money. There is a cost associated with them, but because your money is all invested by computers, the costs are very low (especially when compared to human financial advisors, who aren't any better at investing your money – in fact, they're generally worse).

Housing

One of the big financial decisions that you'll have to make is whether to rent or buy a home. There's an enormous amount of advice out there on this topic – some people will tell you to buy as soon as you can, while others will say that many people should never buy their homes, because houses aren't actually a great investment. The reality is somewhere in between. Owning your home can be a major asset in retirement, and while real estate typically offers lower returns than the stock market does, buying a home has a benefit similar to your 401k – as long as you make your mortgage payment every month, you're automatically saving money without thinking about it.

Because of that, I think home ownership is generally a good idea. It's a more conservative investment than some, but it's okay to be conservative – we're not trying to make you into a billionaire, just make sure that you're going to be able to live a long, happy life with no worries about money. If you've paid off your home and no longer have to make mortgage payments once you retire, that's going to leave you a lot of extra money every month.

That said, there's one rule of thumb that I tend to apply to see if it's a good idea to buy a home – are you pretty confident that you'll live in it for 5 years or more? If that's a yes, then go ahead and buy. If not, it's probably best to continue renting.

If you're curious why, the answer is that there are big costs associated with buying and (especially) selling a home. When you sell your home, you should assume you're going to lose about 8% of the money that you get from the sale to fees and agents' commissions. Here's an example of how that might work against you if you don't live there long enough:

Let's say you buy a house for $200,000. You put down $40,000 for a 20% down payment, plus you spend an extra $5000 in costs, for a total of $45,000 spent up front. You live in it for a year, but then you decide you want to move across the country, so you decide you need to sell it. The real estate market is good, so the value of the house has gone up, and you're able to sell it for $208,000. While it seems like you just made $8000, the reality is that after you pay the costs of selling, you're going to get about $192,000. You pay off what remains of your mortgage, which will be something like $157,000. That leaves you $35,000, which means you lost $10,000 on the house.

This is obviously a situation you want to avoid, which is why I recommend continuing to rent if you're not sure how long you'll be sticking around.

Whether you're renting or buying, it's important to make sure that you aren't spending so much on housing that you're unable to save. The general rule of thumb is not to spend more than 30% of your take-home pay on rent or a mortgage payment. This is a fine starting point, but I recommend taking a bit more time to examine your own situation to find out what the right amount is for you. Ultimately, what really matters is that you're able to pay for your housing and other expenses while still saving money every month. If you have a lot of old debt that you're making payments on every month, you may need to spend less than 30%. On the other hand, if your salary is relatively high, you may be able to spend 40% and still have plenty of room left over to save.

The best approach is to build out your budget (more on this in the next chapter) so that you really understand your costs. Once you know exactly what you're spending every month, it's easy to determine how much is left for rent and a cushion for savings.

One last note on buying vs. renting – if you're not making much money now, but you expect your salary to go up moving forward, you may well be better off renting, even if you're going to stay in the same place. If you have to live somewhere that isn't especially nice for a while in order to save, an apartment is usually the better choice. If you buy a home on a very limited budget, it's probably not going to be in the best shape, which means that repairs are going to come up. If you have a leak in the roof or a burst pipe, that can set you back in a big way if you have to pay for all the costs. Better to rent and let your landlord deal with those things. Beyond that, once you're ready to upgrade to something nicer (though remember that if your income increases you shouldn't spend the whole increase), it's a lot easier to move into a new apartment than it is to sell a house and buy another.

Chapter 11: Tackling Credit Card Debt

The Most Important Rule

When it comes to paying bills (any bill – not just your credit card bills), it is important to remember this: always pay on time. When you don't pay your bills on time, a number of things can happen:

You get charged a late fee. The good news is (yes, there is good news), depending on your history with this particular company, you could call them up ahead of time and tell them that you won't be able to make a payment on time. They might wave the late fee for you. Of course, this won't happen if you're regularly late.

Your interest rate will go up. Did you know that some companies will increase your rate up to 15% after just one late payment? While you've got them on the phone, make sure to ask them about your interest rate and if it will increase because of this. Don't worry about trying to negotiate with them either. Sure, you can't slip him a twenty when you shake hands (I could never perfect that move) but a little ethical negotiation isn't wrong. Ethical negotiation = don't auction off your first born.

It's a ding on your credit report (when your payment is more than a month late). It's incredibly important for you to pay your late amount (and fees) as soon as you can. The longer you wait, the more chance that the company will report your late payment.

Your credit score drops. Did you know that payment history makes up over a third of your credit score? That's why late payments have such a big effect on your overall score. Remember that emergency phone call that you made, to try and avoid that late fee? You can also ask them if this will impact your credit score. A lot of companies won't report a late payment right away (grace periods are awesome and convenient) but don't take their generosity for granted.

Another Important Rule

Okay, I take that back. Paying on time is the most important but at a close second is: Pull your free credit report every year to keep a close eye on your credit score. There are a ton of places that offer free versions of your credit score

Your Credit Card Debt

One of the big ways for you to save money is to tackle your credit card debt. Once you pay off all of those credit cards, you'll have more money to save or to spend on other necessities after all.

Let me tell you my story. I want to preface this story by saying that I spend years paying off my debt and now I am debt free. I did this by utilizing many different methods of cutting back (some of which, I've already mentioned in the previous chapter) and paying off my cards.

I ate out every once in a while, learned that cooking at home can be both cathartic and healthy – not to mention, a great way to spend some time with your loved ones. My husband and I went out on hikes, had plenty of game nights and movie nights at the house, and still had a great time despite the fact that I wasn't dropping thousands of dollars on material goods anymore. Yes, I grew out of that college, "I-have-my-own-money-now" mentality.

Before I go into the specifics of how I personally paid off my credit card debt, let's talk about the two main ways that you can pay off your debt. I want to do this first because your choice should depend on your current situation, not just because I picked Plan A or B.

Snowball Method

The snowball method can be traced back to the famous Dave Ramsey, the financial guru. This method is based on the theory that you should start paying off the smallest balance first. Once you pay that off, you move on to the next one.

Use the money that you would have otherwise been using to pay off the smallest account on top of this regular payment. After that's paid off, do the same with the next one. Use the money that you would have otherwise used on the first two cards to add on to your regular payment.

Not only that, the snowball method also helps build your confidence as you pay off your smaller debts. Because you can see progress faster, you feel better about saving money and paying off your debts. It feels good to see that progress.

Avalanche Method

This method requires that you list off your credit card (or other) debts by interest rate. Place the largest interest rate first and descend down from that. Pay off the debt with the highest interest rate first. This makes it so you will pay off your debt faster and you spend less money on just plain interest.

This plan makes a lot of sense logically but you have to have some strong will-power to really stick to your plan.

What did I do?

My situation: I had a few credit cards that I had to pay off, all with various balances. I was also working two part time jobs, in addition to going to school full time to get my bachelor's degree. I was busy. I was also very tired.

I had accrued this debt because I wasn't informed when I started getting credit card offers in the mail. Because of that, I was irresponsible. Luckily for me, I could fix my mistakes and so can you, no matter your situation. You just have to find the right process.

I chose the Snowball Method – opting to pay off my department store cards first (because they had the smallest balances) and then worked my way up to the bigger accounts. I chose this one because - while my debt was significant - I was still young and didn't quite have the willpower that I needed to choose the latter of the two.

Your Credit Score Is Important.

There are many different ways to mess up your credit score. Here are three big ways for you to mess up your credit without even trying:

Use up Your Available Credit.

Yep, there are other ways to destroy your credit card too – and this is one of them. Don't take their $15,000 credit limit as a challenge. Your credit utilization ratio (how much credit you're actually using) is extremely influential in figuring out what your credit score is.

So if you have $15,000 of available credit and you use up $14,999, you could be doing your credit card and your credit score harm. The best ratios are 10% or lower but on average, you should aim for about 30%.

Maxing Out More Than One Card

Not only is this a great way to destroy a credit card, it'll also do a number on your credit score. This ruins your credit score because it messes with your credit utilization ratio – like when you use up your available credit by maxing out a card. Just imagine what will happen if you max out more than one of your cards.

Closing Your Highest Limit Card First

Remember credit utilization ratio I talked about at number one? Consider this: you've got a card with a $20,000 limit and one with a $2,000 limit. All together, you've got $22,000 of available credit. Even if you've got a $3,000 dollar balance on the card with the highest limit, and $1,000 on the smaller card - that still leaves you with $17,000 of credit and a credit utilization ratio of about 22%.

Okay, let's say that you pay off and close out the card with the highest limit. That knocks your available credit to only

$2,000. Your ratio then skyrockets to 50% and your credit score won't like that number.

Things You Should Know About Credit Cards

Having been in the situation where I didn't know what I was doing when I first acquired my first credit card, I found that knowledge is one of the best things you can arm yourself with.

Having a credit card doesn't mean that you have to use it or be in debt.

It isn't black and white. You don't have to keep it locked up or be forever in debt. There are other ways of using credit cards. It is totally possible for you to use your credit card regularly and stay out of debt by charging only what you can afford to pay when the bill arrives each month. Of course, in order to do this, you have to make sure that you keep a close eye on how much you are spending.

You can easily create a repayment plan by yourself or with the aid of creditors (though it would be nice not to have to get them involved).

Unlike popular belief, companies really do want you to pay them back. They don't want you forever in debt. Creditors and collection companies will work with you in order to develop a repayment plan. You can even work with a credit counselor if you need some advice on coming up with a plan that gets you out of the red but still allows for you to live a fun and healthy life.

You can't go to jail for nonpayment but they can take a lot from you.

If you have credit card debt and you don't pay it off, you won't go to prison. However, the companies can sue you and garnish your wages and/or assets as the judge sees fit.

If you don't pay on time, there are a bunch of hidden fees to watch out for.

Let's say that you close a credit card account without actually looking at the final statement. That little balance can grow into a gigantic monster because of late fees, interest, and default APR. Not only that, there is a specific residual interest that is generated after the bill is issued and before your payment is actually received. If you can, always pay your balance in full, all the time. Don't stop making payments after you close the account.

Don't go applying for every credit card out there.

Having credit available all the time is good for your credit score so the theory stands that if you can get a credit card, you should apply for it, right? Wrong. Every time you apply for a credit card and you get rejected, it's a ding on your credit score.

Double your sign up bonus.

Sign up bonuses can be great and they don't always come around so have your spouse or partner apply for the same card s you in order to double up on those bonuses. Just make sure that you keep a close eye on how much you spend. Just because those bonuses are there, doesn't mean that they will be there forever and that you can't overspend.

Gift cards can be used in creative ways too.

If you need to reach a minimum spending threshold in order to get a sign up bonus, use your credit card to purchase gift cards for stores that you visit often. You can even use your credit card to buy cash cards. Just make sure that you buy the cards before the deadline. Then you can use the gift cards later. Here's another trick. If you get bonus points on your card for shopping at certain places, like your local grocery store, buy your gift cards there to get the points, get the sign up bonus, and have the gift cards to use later.

Chapter 12: Financial Planning:

Financial planning is simply about everything and anything that has a direct or indirect impact on your financial situation, either in the present or in the future. Simply put, it is nearly everything that you do or intend to do. Sadly, many people mistakenly think that financial planning is about just the money. However, money is simply the beginning.

In order to critically understand this, we need to know what money is in the first place.

What is Money?

Anything that is accepted as payment for goods, products and services is considered as money. With reference to current society, it is usually in the form of paper currency and coins. In the past, as we see in history, everything from coffee beans to gold and diamonds, and even salt was used as money. While the contents used have changed, the concept it represents is something that hasn't changed since the invention of the barter system.

Money simply is a representation of anything with value. Typically, if you had, say 10 million dollars, then the amount of paper currency you technically own symbolizes that you have an inherent large amount of value. This money can represent anything from cars, to houses, gadgets to food. All that is left is for you to act on that value, and spend it.

You might wonder how this is linked to financial planning. In simple words, everything is linked to financial planning. Anything that deals with your money, how you spend it, save it or splurge it – all these plans are simply financial planning. It can include planning on how you're going to spend your money on everything from food, to vacations to transport, careers, entertainment, and business. Financial planning basically includes every single thing that involves the exchange of money.

What's the Point?

The point is quite clear if you pay attention. It simply isn't about how to hoard as much as possible, or to buy as much as possible. That bit would be outright silly. Financial planning is about creating an ideal plan to utilize your material wealth to fit into what you want to do and who it is that you want to be. Simples.

For most people, this would indicate that a traditional job won't really work out. For a few, the monotony of a day-night desk job simply doesn't fit the bill. For a few more, relaxing and chilling doesn't really work out. My mindset is such that unless I have a major project – not corporate wise – just something that utilizes the majority of my time; I feel completely wasted and incomplete. There simply is no satisfaction in what I want to do at that stage. For others, it can be quite different.

Remember that financial planning simply isn't a one-for-all affair. It needs to be custom tailored to your individual needs and requirements. It is simply the planning out of your life.

In circumstances where life is never always certain, not everyone is completely secure. If anyone tells you otherwise, they're either lying to you, or have a secret gold/diamond mine stashed away from the world. Most of the people I know are not prepared completely for heading into retirement. It is simply a necessity for that stage of their lives.

Which brings us to the question at hand. How can I write one?!

Given below is a step by step by step guide to begin writing your own plan. While this is not set in stone, you have flexibility to customize it to make it personal to you. I've tried to list out all the major issues that your plan will ideally need to handle head on.

Establish Your Goals

First of all, figure out what exactly it is that you want in your life. Think about what kind of life it is that you want to lead. Think about where it is that you see yourself, the size of your house, the type of education that you want to have, or want your kids to have, the number of pets – everything that is linked to money in the remotest of ways. Don't hesitate to dream, figure out what you want. You Live Only Once!

Write these thoughts down on paper. There's something about setting your thoughts down that makes your goal come one step closer to you.

Write down each and every one of these details. Add to them as you keep thinking of things. Remember to keep it realistic. Create your dream as a physical reality on a sheet of paper. Once you have the basics written down, add the "mundane" details – insurance, bills, a clean kitchen, a well stocked pantry – everything and anything that is needed for a full home.

Ideally, your plan should include each of the following:

Education:

Additional education is always possible. The majority of the world lives under the misconception that it is only the young who can go to college; however, I have had the privilege of attending university with some people who are well into their 70's. Their reason (with a smile of course), is that you are never too old to stop learning!

Remember, it is all about your goals – what do you want to learn more? Is it necessary to help you achieve your other goals? Everything is under its purview. That said, it is also necessary to remember that you might want to consider your children's education (if you want to pay for it, that is).

Occupation:

With consideration to your occupation — know what field you want to work with. Would you like to work a typical 9 – 5 work? Do you want to have your own business? Do you want to be part of a creative industry and economy? Do you want to have a passive source of income? The purpose

What field do you -want- to work in? Do you want a typical 9-5? Do you want to work in the creative economy? Do you want your own business? Do you want to build a passive income? Remember, the purpose of your job is financial happiness.

Lifestyle:

Drawing on the same concepts as that of your occupation, how do you foresee yourself spending your life? Do you plan on making all other aspects of your life revolve around work? Are you comfortable with a seemingly simple lifestyle? Do you want to have a lot of activities and interests? What car or vehicle do you want to drive?

Remember that every single step or stage costs you money, and this needs to be taken into consideration. Make calculations on how much you need to make in order to achieve all your targets. Research is essential, and can be a bit of a drag; but this research done now, will help you plan towards the future you want.

Residence:

This section asks the obvious questions – where do you see yourself living? It is absolutely not necessary to live where you are right now. Some prefer the country, some the mountains, some the city, and some near/on a beach. Once you've landed there, the next question that begs answering is what size you want your home to be.

Research this information online to know how much it is you'd be looking to spend. Be realistic in your goals. Know what you want and how much you want to spend.

Retirement:

Once you've made the plans for the above, you will then need to consider what you want to do in your retirement. Where do you want to live, how do you want to live, who do you want to live with? Family or friends, on your own or in a retirement community? Know what you want.

Insurance:

As clichéd as it sounds, the only certainty in life is that nothing is every certain. Remember that you need to be secure in case of any and all emergencies, and insurance is a critical component to financial security. Each plan needs to have in consideration, a provision for insurance.

The majority of the chances are usually in your favor, and it actually costs much less than you think in order to achieve your life's goals. Even with a high-flying, vacation-every-month plan, the amount of expenditure you need to achieve your goals is relatively short.

The internet is awash with articles that offer guidance to show that a little bit can often go a whole lot further than we have thought. Do your research, I can promise you that it will change your life. Your dreams are perhaps quite cheap and there are websites in the thousands that offer advice on how to live on a literal shoe string budget.

Where life hacks and how-to-save money hacks are the norm, there is no friend better than the internet. Learn to search smart, read as much as you can on what your planned activity is. There is probably someone in the world, who has already done what you want, in cheap and effective manner, and published it on the internet!

Plan Your Income

It is always a bit to consider, that your plans aren't just about the dreams you have. You have to also shell out some hard-earned cash to achieve it. This, sadly, is the bit that most people find hard to get used to. Most planning books are often always designed on the single core principle that you'll be in love with the job you're currently doing for the rest of your life.

While some people find it quite easy to continue in the same path, you'll find that people change their jobs all the time. Some start freelancing, others start work on their own businesses, or begin other methods that offer new

Financial planning is something that you will have to start off as a young adult, probably as you enter the middle of your college life. If you haven't done so already, well, you don't need to worry! This book and the ideas inside are based on principles that will help you figure it all out! You will need to know where you intend to make your money from.

In all honesty, don't step in expecting to rake in the big bucks right from the start. The moolah will come to you, eventually. If you take smart choices, budget and plan your way across your chosen professional field, you'll be able to make the best of your income no matter what stage or step of the ladder you're climbing.

Among the sources of income, the most popular ones are:

Career:

Fortunately or unfortunately, the drill is more or less the same – head off to college, get a proper job, which means you start at the bottom and work your way up a greased flag pole to reach your success. This is on the whole, a proper idea with of course, the exceptional cases. The majority of the crowd who need an effective financial plan always have to emphasize on what their career will be while planning.

Business:

Recent polls (Harris polls) have now shown that up to 72% of the people who are of an employable age are considering beginning their own enterprise. You really don't need a fancy MBA or a degree from a management university, and its allied connections and what not to get started on your own, especially in the internet age. You can do everything from a gardening care consultancy, to writing content for a website, to coordinating holidays and tour packages in your city. The internet is your friend, and the possibilities are limitless!

Investing:

One of the most positive and powerful ways to increase your wealth is investment, and the key reason is simply because investment focuses on increasing your existing wealth exponentially as opposed to obtaining new wealth. This can be done in different forms – investing in the stock market, buying some real estate, gold or even getting a new degree! Remember that it simply makes more sense to put your money into a bank account that gets you a percentage of interest that simply letting the money sit uselessly gathering dust.

Chapter 13: Monitoring Progress And Making Adjustments

Tracking is necessary to ensure that the strategies you chose will be effective and that each person included in the budgeting plan is actually doing his or her part. The first step in tracking your progress is to break down your goal to smaller chunks.

Break down big targets to smaller ones

For bigger target amounts, you may need to break down your saving goal. By breaking big budgeting goals down, you will not be intimidated by the size of the goal. Each breakdown should be considered a small victory, a milestone if you will.

If you need to save $10,000 for example, you can break down the goal into five $2,000 milestones. Instead of focusing on $10,000, you just need to set your mind to reach the next $2,000.

Set a timeline on when you will reach each milestone

Now that you have broken your goal down to smaller, more manageable mini-goals, the next step is to anticipate how long it will take you to reach each mini-goal. If you are saving $500 each payday, for example, and you have two paydays each month, you should be able to reach the $2,000-mark by the fourth payday or the second month.

You should mark the days when you will reach each of these goal milestones in your calendar. This will help motivate you to work harder for the next milestone. It may also help if you make use of a progress bar in your phone to remind yourself of your budgeting progress. Goal setting apps usually have these types of feature to remind you of your goal and the progress you've made.

Identify the behaviors that lead to better budgeting performance

Now that you are actually implementing your plan, you will have a better idea of the strategies that work and the ones that do not. You will need to identify these behaviors and maximize the behaviors that do help you save money better.

Sometimes, you may realize that your strategy is not fast enough for your goal deadline. This may mean that you will need to adjust your behavior some more to improve your performance. One way to do this is by cutting back some more in some areas. If this is not possible, you may also choose to improve your income instead of cutting back. By increasing your income, you will be able to increase the amount that you can put into your savings.

Choose your tools

Aside from the tools discussed in earlier chapters for tracking your spending, you can also make use of a ledger where you put all the information about your daily expenses and your savings. You can choose to keep your ledger in your home or your office. You should update your ledger daily or weekly to keep track of your daily spending and your budgeting progress.

If you are used to using a smartphone, there are apps that you can use to keep track of your spending. Apps like Monefy acts like a notepad where you can put all the information about your spending habits. You can then export the data in the file into a spreadsheet file that you can use to act as a ledger.

These tools will help you get the bird's eye view of how effective your budgeting strategies are. When it comes to money, everything can be measured through numbers. If the numbers show that you are falling short of your savings expectations, this means that changes need to be made in your strategies.

Make everything clear and update your progress

Your entire budgeting operation needs to be simple if you wish it to be successful. To start, your goals and the strategies that you will use should be clear to the people involved in the budgeting process. Each step that needs to be taken should be laid out for everyone to see. If there is a habit that needs to be developed, you must make sure that everybody is aware of it and that everyone knows of the steps that must be taken to develop that habit.

If you wish to lessen your electricity bill for example, each member of the household may need to develop a habit of turning off every unused electrical item in the house before leaving the house or before sleeping.

Kids and teens however, may not be aware of all the appliances that they need to check. To develop the habit among these members of the household, you can put up a list of all the things that they need to turn off when they leave or when they go to sleep. Show them how to use it so that they will also follow your example.

You can also make the goal and the plan clearer to the rest of the people involved in the budgeting process if you have a progress bar of your budgeting that everyone can check out. You can make a simple progress bar with the timeline to the goal on a piece of paper. You can then update this tool every time the family saves money and adds the saved money to the goal fund. If you show that all the hard work and sacrifices are making progress, you will be able to motivate everybody else to keep doing what they are already doing.

It is common for people who do not have a clear view of the goal and the progress to feel fatigue with all the budgeting. They get tired of always holding back in their spending. If these people are used to spending their money freely or to having a bigger budget, they may feel bad with the budgeting process. By putting a progress bar somewhere everyone can see it, they may feel that all their sacrifices and all the difficulties they are going through are bearing some fruit.

Reinforce positive behavior

When you see someone in your family doing their part in implementing the budgeting plan, praise them for it. Praising, when done at the right time, can remind the people who are budgeting with you that they are doing the right thing. By showing that you appreciate that they are following the plan, they are more likely to do the same behavior again in the future.

When you and your family reach a milestone in your budgeting, you should set some money aside to celebrate. The celebration does not need to be expensive. It may just be a special home cooked meal.

Chapter 14: Saving Money

The next step in managing your personal finances is to save money. When you start utilizing the tactics in the last chapter you will notice a difference in how much you are spending on things you normally buy every month.

When you start to become creative in how you can buy the things you still want and need for a smaller amount, you will want to put the money you are saving into your bank savings account.

For example, if you normally spend or set a $500 limit on groceries every month and you start utilizing tactics to cut costs and you find out that you now get the same groceries you usually get for $480, then you will put in the $20 you save every month into your savings account. Now, $20 may not seem like much but you will want to have pride that you are able to save any amount of money, even with debt.

Other ways you can utilize to start saving money or obtaining more money to save, is by selling items in your house you no longer need or grew out of. You can sell these items in a yard sales or sell them online. The point is you will want to sell things you know you no longer will use again, or items you grew out of.

You can also utilize any gift cards people give you especially items that can be used for items you need for your household and purchase with the gift cards instead of cash. The money you save there can also be transferred to your savings account.

If you also notice that you eat out for lunch every day while at work, instead take a lunch to work and save the money you didn't spend by eating out or buy one less coffee every day.

Other tips you can utilize to save money can be:

Yard sale or sell items you no longer need or want online

Carpool to work

Use gift cards you are given to buy household items instead

Use Coupons and promo codes to cut costs

Eat out less

Take up a side job on weekends

Practice Good driver habits to get discounted insurance rates or a rebate check

If you have a card with rewards features, use your card to buy household items and then quickly pay the bill

Use rebate saving apps to redeem points for gift cards

Contribute to company's 401K to save money without being taxed (keep in mind your after tax income may be less).

Save your pocket change and pick up pennies/change people just lay around

Buy household items especially if they are on the clearance items at your favorite stores

Buy generic brands of your favorite items – Trust me, they are the same as the name brands

Buy in Bulk, you need to calculate this before purchasing but buying in bulk can lead to cost savings.

Buy gas at stations that are partnered with grocery stores. Usually the grocery stores will give you gas discounts. Sometimes these discounts can be at much as 50cents off per gallon, which will add up over time.

When you start to cut costs, you will notice that the money you will save will add up over time. In time you can take half of what you are saving and use the money to start paying off debts.

In the next chapter, we will cover the proper way to slowly get out of debt.

Chapter 15: Creating A Budget

Coming up with a budget may seem daunting at first, but this chapter will walk you through every step of the entire process to make it seamless.

1. Why Do You Want To Create A Budget?

People who budget are almost two times less likely to suffer any financial anxiety as compared to spenders, and they're less likely to live from wage to wage or struggle with finances.

While budgeting is a good practice for anyone, it is important that you identify your goals before beginning the process because the reasons why you have decided to start budgeting may influence the choices you make as you design the budget.

While thinking about your motivations may seem silly, psychology is a big factor in how you decide to handle money. In fact, a research paper published by Berkeley's GGSC shows that the process of coming up with a budget will make it more likely for you to achieve your goals because the process of crunching the numbers discourages overspending, enhances motivation and creates an emotional investment.

Let us learn more about setting budgeting goals since, as mentioned earlier, if you have set certain goals, you are likely to stick to your budget since you know what you are working towards.

Setting Financial Goals

Budgeting effectively entails being able to set certain financial goals and using that budget as a tool to help you achieve those goals. You can set simple goals such as saving enough money in a few months to buy tickets to a movie premiere or grand goals such as saving enough money to retire at 50. Sometimes you could even have two or more goals that you are working towards.

Other reasons for coming up with a budget could include:

Reduce or get out of debt

Avoid spending money you don't have

Breaking the wage to wage cycle

Ensuring that your spending habits reflect your values and goals

Putting an end to money squabbles for couples

Cutting down on overspending on problem areas

Staying on track toward short and long-term financial goals

As a way to save more money

Proper budgeting will make it easy for you to establish your short and long term goals and track your progress and enable them to become a reality.

When setting your financial goals, it is imperative to follow the SMART acronym. Let us evaluate this further

Specific: You need to be very specific about your financial goals and what you hope the budget to achieve. For instance, instead of saying, "I want to a budget to help me stop overspending," have a more specific reason such as, "I want a budget to help me stop overspending on clothes and only spend X amount of money." If you want to save more, you can have a goal such as, "I want to be able to save X amount of money every month." Ensure that your goals are as specific as possible so that you know what you are working towards.

Measurable: How will you know that you are achieving your goals unless you can measure them. Ensure that whatever goals you set, you can measure the progress to see if you are moving in the right direction or not.

Achievable: The financial goals you set need to be achievable to enable you to come up with ways of achieving the goals, or else you will be frustrated chasing something you cannot achieve. While the goal should be achievable, it should also challenge you so that you get out of your comfort zone and stretch your limits.

Relevant: You need to do a lot of soul-search to ensure that you set goals that are important to you and align with your core values and purpose or else you will end up setting goals to please others or to remain relevant only to regret later because it is not something that you really wanted.

Time-bound: Your goals need to have time limits. You cannot just set a goal within a set period within which to achieve the goal. This is where having short term and long-term financial goals come in.

Short-term financial goals: A short term goal is a goal that you would want to achieve in less than two years. The essence of these goals is to get your finances in order by getting rid of credit card debt and setting up your emergency fund. Other short term financial goals could include making some minor home improvements, buying new household appliances, saving for a car down payment, etc.

Long-term financial goals: These entail goals that you would want to achieve in five years or more. Such goals require you to take methodical planning (effective budgeting) to achieve. One of the common long-term financial goals for most people is saving adequate to retire comfortably. Other long-term financial goals you could have include paying your student loan, paying off a mortgage, traveling the word etc.

Achieving long-term financial goals is usually challenging because sometimes the future seems far off. To ensure you remain on track, you can use some online calculators to know how much you need to set aside to achieve those goals. A good example is the online long-term savings calculator. This tool allows you to key in your variables such as your current age, expected rate of return on your investment, and amount currently saved among others to find out how much you have to save every month to realize your long term goal.

Beware that some online calculators yield varied results. As such, try a few of them to get a general idea for the amount you need to save. At this point, it is important that you begin to view these figures you save every month as non-negotiable monthly expenses. If completely necessary, also adjust other expenditure categories as required to create room for the new savings category.

In addition to using online calculators, you can opt to use automatic saving. Sometimes, we are just too busy and we forget about the saving commitments we have made. To ensure this does not happen and you achieve your financial goals, set up automatic deductions that go into the appropriate saving accounts that you have set up.

2. Calculate Your Total Income

Budgeting is supposed to help you make use of your earnings more efficiently. That's why you need to know how much money you make every month. Factor in your total earnings from all sources. These should capture wage income, all income from investments, business earnings, child support, and/or alimony and money from side hustles.

If your monthly income is unpredictable, consider paying yourself a salary first. In other words, decide on an invariable figure to base your budget around so that you may save any extra money you make. This constant figure could be based on what you would usually make in a bad month (if you want to reduce the chances of overspending while building a bigger cushion) or what you normally earn on average.

3. Be Realistic About Your Expenditure

You need to identify what your existing spending habits are before coming up with a realistic budget. Any budget you create will be nothing more but a wish list if it isn't practical. The moment you identify where all your money is going is the moment you will know whether your budget is realistic. It is advisable to track your expenses for about a month to get a clear picture of all your expenses. The following are three methods you can use to track your expenses:

By use of statements

Bank and credit card statements can help you track your spending habits. However, this approach may not produce very detailed results since you may not be in a position to recall what a specific transaction was for. Nevertheless, going back over a month or more of statements might immediately get you started with your budget as it paints a general picture that you can use as a starting point.

Use of mobile apps

Some innovative apps, such as PocketGuard, Dollarbird, and Mint, ease the burden of tracking since it links your bank accounts and your credit cards. Make sure that you connect all the accounts you own to ascertain that every purchase is labeled appropriately to have an accurate assessment.

Record your expenditure on a notebook or spreadsheet

This is the most practical approach of the three; however, it can be a time-consuming process as well. Whenever you spend money on anything, put it down on paper or input it in a spreadsheet. Make sure you record all expenses immediately after the transaction before you forget the figures. Also, do not get rid of your receipts.

4. Don't Forget Insurance

As you come up with your monthly expenses, don't forget to include insurance. Disasters and accidents are part and parcel of our everyday life, and if you are not adequately insured, your finances face the prospect of getting ruined.

The purpose of insurance is to protect your life and that of your family, keep a roof over your head and maintain your ability to continue earning income. Life insurance, homeowners' insurance, and disability insurance can help with the above situations.

It is now up to you to decide what kind of life insurance you need based on your financial needs.

5. Choose An Appropriate Budgeting System

The best approach to budgeting will depend on what you aim to achieve. Do you want to save more or pay down debt or do you simply want to curb overspending? All the budgeting systems we learned earlier are designed to help you evaluate and understand your relationship with money. While they may share a common goal, they usually use different strategies to get there. You'll just have to choose one that makes sense for you.

Here are a few things to consider to choose the most suitable budgeting approach:

How long have you budgeting

If this is the very first time you are looking to create a budget, then the 50/30/20 budget rule is the most suitable one or you. What makes this method attractive for the beginners is that it splits your earnings across the three major categories, including needs, necessities, and savings. As such, it gives you plenty of room to help settle your debt, cover current costs, and save for the future. You can use this system by itself or as a starting point/basis to create a flexible budget that suits your situation.

Want to make the most of every penny

If you are a meticulous planner or one who tends to overspend, the Zero Based Budget should address both needs. This strategy makes spending and monitoring clear. After earning your income, it will need you to use every dollar in a premeditated way. This avoids instances of overspending because every dollar has something to do.

You desire to control your spending

If you simply want to stay out of debt or decrease the rate of frivolous spending but don't want to track every dollar you spend, then you need a rigid system such as the envelope budgeting system. This method will allow you to set a limit for every expense category, like utilities and groceries, fill the envelopes with the allotted money, and use that cash for those particular expenses. When the money in a specific envelope runs out, you won't be able to spend more on that category until the following month, and this helps instill some kind of financial discipline if you have been spending aimlessly.

You want to put up some savings

If your sole interest in budgeting is to build up savings, the Pay Yourself First strategy will help you achieve that goal. This budgeting approach is primarily designed to align your values and spending, and it is no surprise that it prioritizes savings before other immediate expenses. After you earn your paycheck, this system lets you decide how much money you want to set aside for goals such as an emergency fund or retirement. The remainder you can now use for other costs, including bills.

6. Have A Household Meeting

If you have a partner, get them on board since budgeting is a team project. But if you are single, you don't have to worry about that. Getting your significant other involved is important because, according to a survey by SunTrust Bank, 35% of respondents in a relationship or partnership felt that money was the main cause of relationship wrangles.

As you have the conversation about money, make it easy for your spouse to take part in the discussion actively. Begin with the basic aspects of a budget that cover bills like utilities, groceries, and gas. Then move on to how both of you will choose to spend the discretionary earnings on things like shopping, eating out, and what other individual expenses should be.

To make things even much easier, you can consider breaking your monthly income into weekly amounts for easier management of your money. This way, once the money is all used up, both of you will have to cease spending. As the end of the month approaches, go back and revisit the budget and compare it with how you both spent the money. This approach, especially when both of you are actively taking part in the budgeting process, can lift some of the pressure off your family and help prevent fights that could potentially accompany every expenditure.

7. Keep Track Of Every Expense, No Matter How Small

When you have finally settled on the budgeting strategy to use, how do you begin using it? Some payments, such as mortgages or rent, are easy to remember. However, for other miscellaneous expenses, you'll need to save receipts. If you feel that's too tedious, you can record all your expenses on the same credit and debit card to keep the process of recording easy. However, it is important to note that the descriptions of the transactions on your credit card statement will not always be 100% clear, and this may leave you wondering what exactly that $20.13 purchase could be.

Alternatively, you can use tangible cash for the little miscellaneous expenses. Ensure that you have some money on you by withdrawing a specific amount on a weekly or monthly basis. Categorize this in your budget as 'miscellaneous.' While this approach might prevent you from overspending, it might not paint the clearest picture yet of where each of your dollars is ending up.

Here are some tips to help you track your expenses:

Update your budget every day

Tracking your money daily takes minimal time, and it also ensures that you don't forget any expenditures.

Use precise descriptions

Put down all your expenses in writing by what they are instead of where you purchased them. This way, you'll be able to find out how much money you spend in a particular category. For instance, if you eat out at McDonald's or Starbucks, you might make orders that include a coke, iced coffee, burgers, or salads. If you simply list all the orders under McDonald's, you really won't know where your $100 went.

8. Reward Yourself

If your budget is only tailored to come up with savings only meant for dreary activities such as saving for the unexpected medical bills and car repairs or for paying off debt, your only incentive for saving is the fear of what comes next if you don't. While fear can serve as a great motivator, constantly being on fear mode is no fun at all.

That said, even if your debt has reached rock bottom and you are committed to digging yourself out as soon as possible, you could also do yourself some good by including some rewards into your savings initiative.

That said, it's important to ensure that you reward yourself for the successes you achieve. Build reward systems into your monthly budget. For instance, if you adhere to your budget for a couple of months, set money aside, for a movie or a dinner with your spouse or best friend. After a few more months, set aside some money for a nice vacation. In so doing, you are making the budgeting process into a game of sorts where you reward yourself for practicing good financial behavior.

The thing with budgeting is that it is not set on stone; it is important to realize when things are not going as planned and adapting. Let us learn more about adjusting your budget in the following chapter.

Chapter 16: Prepare A Budget

What a good budget should be like.

It should motivate you to spend less and to save more.

What you should do.

Make your budget easy on the eyes

How

Hide or delete any items you don't want to see on the expenditure list next month or moving forward.

Make the amount of savings big enough to see how it grows each month and moving forward.

In your future expenditure list, include a column where you can place the amount of money you've saved as a result of cutting costs in a specific category.

Prepare a Budget

This is where you create a new budget. You now know your spending history; you already have established trends, determined points where costs can be cut, eliminated items, and so on. Look at the resulting data now. If everything left is something you need, create another spreadsheet that contains the same rows, columns, and items as the previous file. Apply money allocations to each item based on your estimates and on your present income. And moving forward, determine who much money you've spent on each item and under each category. You'll be surprised at the results and how much insights are present by looking at your previous spending history.

Chapter 17: Tax Payment 101

America is a great country to live, but paying taxes is not a good option. It has a higher tax rate than many Asian countries. There are different schemes to avoid paying more tax. If you know how to pay less in taxes, you can save more, and it will eventually help with debt management. This segment deals with basics of paying taxes. Each year you have to fill a self-assessment form or a tax return form. Boring it may seem, but reading that form saves you from many penalties and fines. Mostly, you'll get the assessment form near 6th April.

Why do I have to fill that form?

· You are working as a freelancer, or you have business partnerships.

· You are approaching the cut point for basic tax level.

· You have multiple income sources.

· You are director of your company.

· You own a land or property.

· You get capital gains from investments.

· You have oversea earnings.

There can be multiple reasons that the form was sent to you. Traditionally, when you submit the tax form, you get three documents from the HMRC.

Tax return

It is a 10-page form that requires basic information submission from you.

Tax return guide

It is a comprehensive document (36 pages) guiding you how to fill the tax return form.

Tax calculation guide

This guide lets you calculate the rebate amount in an easy way.

Depending on your country/income/responsibilities, it can be a pretty difficult time filling the form. HMRC also sends supplementary pages relating to individual requirements. It is your duty to fill every tax form. You can contact the HMRC representative to get information. Make a phone call, direct appointment or attend a Skype meeting. Make sure that no tax is left unpaid.

You may not have to fill the assessment form if:

· You receive payment from one employer under the "PAYE".

· You do not have an extraordinary income, so you only pay taxes through the PAYE system regularly.

Avoid these common mistakes

· Sign the form after filling the required information.

· Check all the "essential boxes" and tick the right answer.

· Provide clear information about any due payment.

· Do not forget to tick your repayment choice.

· Put the bank account numbers where required.

· Attach all supplementary pages and correctly fill the relevant ones.

Read the "tax return guide" to gain further information and help.

Writing about savings & investments

Your tax return documents also require you to write about your savings & investments. You'll get an annual report for all investments. Here are some points to note:

The annuity provider gives you the details about which portion of the payment is tax-free.

There will be some discounted securities. These can be stock market index trading bonds and capital investment trust shares.

This book is written as a general concept. The tax paying rules & documents are different for every country. Reading the balance sheet, tax documents, and tax return forms is a basic financial education. We all should be familiar with these concepts. As a good rule, we all should get an introductory course on major life subjects i.e. world economics, accounting, physics, mathematics, business, relationships, and biology. We do not have to be the expert, but learning an introductory college course will help.

Debt Consolidation

Warren Buffet once said, "there is one way to make more money, do not lose anything." Paying your debt is not like 2+2=4. It is a different story. You have to be really good at what you do. Debt can be qualified as both good & bad types. Businesses take loans, and they make huge profits on this loan. It seems like you are very unfortunate to be in debt, but you can create luck out of this situation. It is possible to learn from your mistakes and mark a new era in your financial history.

Most times, paying the debt is not difficult if you have a flat amount to pay. Loan interest rate is a terrible option, and we have to do something about it. It becomes impossible to pay the debt when you are paying 20% interest rate every month. One option is to reduce the interest rate. Debt management firms do this for you by closing the credit card. It does have a negative impact on credit history, but it significantly reduces the interest rate.

Debt consolidation is another option. It simply means to take another debt to pay your current debt. You use a flat amount to pay multiple monthly debts. If done right, this option can significantly reduce your interest rate. How do we do that? It depends on how much you owe to the creditors and what is your financial situation. It is recommended to consult a financial expert who can better analyze individual situations. Do you consider yourself broke? It might be difficult to get a bank loan, but this is the option you should choose.

Here are some reasons to choose debt consolidation:

· The interest rate on new debt is lower than the current interest rate you pay. Let's say the interest on credit card debt is 15%, and the bank loan asks for an interest rate of 10%. In such a condition, debt consolidation can improve the situation.

· You do not have to settle for a variable interest rate. Variable interest rate starts with a small amount but continues to build up since the creditor asks for interest on the interest amount.

· You can pay the new debt quickly since you are saving some money on the interest rate. You also experience freedom since you paid previous multiple debts. Now, you have to focus your energy in one direction.

· You must also commit that you'll not take any new debt unless the bank loan has been cleared.

Debt consolidation seems the right option for many, but many people are ignorant when dealing with financial issues. You give them money, and they start getting into more debt. The problem can be with their health or spending habits. Some people never pay the previous debts and for them debt consolidation is just new debt and some negative score on credit history.

There are several options to consolidate your debt like:

· Transfer the credits from a high-interest credit card to a lower interest credit card rate.

· Bank loan

· Borrow against the life insurance policy.

· Borrow from your retirement account

These are all difficult options to consider. Especially, taking funds from your retirement account seems a very tough situation to handle. Talk to your personal finance expert and see which option can be best for you.

Transferring balance

Transferring the balance from a high-interest credit card to the one with lower interest rate seems like the right option, but it is the one that comes with trouble. You can use the current credit card with a lower interest rate, or you can shop for a new one. Each card comes with tiny details printed in a small font. Take your magnifying glass and start reading the text. The text tells that the debt interest rate may jump quite higher if your payment is one day late. It may also tell different figures about shopping new products. The company policy may change from time to time, and so does the interest rate. Read those tiny details before you decide anything.

Here are some tips:

Calculate the interest rate on an offer and ask 'how long will that interest rate last?' When you transfer funds, you may get a lower interest rate, but the offer expires very soon, and you are again in the same situation. You do not have the option to transfer debts again from one card to the other. It gives you reduced interest rate, but will badly hurt your credit history and credit score.

Some rules are associated with the interest rate. Ignore those rules and the interest rate is going to jump higher. If you are late with payments, you are going to face penalties and eventually a higher interest rate.

Understand the meaning of universal default clause. If you consolidate debt with a card that uses the universal default clause, the credit company can increase the interest rate anytime if they found late payment records, or you took a lot of new debts. Why is this clause so dangerous?

Universal default rate simply means that the company can charge you the default interest rate if you do something wrong. It is just like that you are late with the payment on your Mastercard, and the interest rate on the visa card jumps. Read on and I have some surprising facts about the universal default clause. If the interest rate jumps, it is more likely to be late with payments. You get late with a payment and the universal default clause again comes into action resulting in skyrocketing interest rate. The creditor charges you more if you have late payments with other lenders. The law is taking notice of this clause, but most credit card companies still use it. So, how do you know if the credit card uses the universal default clause? The tiny text on the credit card will look similar to this one:

"We may change the rates, fees, and terms of your account at any time for any reason. These reasons may be based on information in your credit reports, such as your failure to make payments to another creditor when due, amounts owed, or the number of credit inquiries. . ."

Depending on your debt value, companies will charge a fee for a debt transfer. You may be charged a flat value or a percentage of your total debt amount.

The companies use several methods to calculate monthly payments. Purchase the card that uses average daily balance method to determine monthly payments. Please also note the grace period. Cards have a 20, 25 or 30 days grace period. Beware of new purchases you make. The interest rate bounces up everytime you make a new purchase.

Bank Loan

Our 2nd option is to take a bank loan. The problem is to get attractive interest rates. The book will evaluate your financial situation to determine if you qualify for a bank loan. There are some ways to consolidate debt through the bank loan. You can pau debts against the equity in your home or the loan to finance your mortgage. Take your time and visit around to see which lender offers you the best policy. Some provide best interest rate while others will be more willing to work with you.

Our desire is to get an unsecured debt consolidation loan. An unsecured debt does not allow the bank to put a lien on your assets. The lender may tell that the only way to get a debt is to have a family member co-sign the note. Do not ever do it. It is just too risky and embarrassing. Let's imagine you cannot repay the loan and then the bank will pressurize your family member/friend to pay the money. Do not put them in the same situation as you are. You can ask them to help you with a loan without any interest rate. That'll be helpful, but do not ask them to co-sign the note. It is like getting your family into a big disaster.

Taking loan against your home equity

Now, this can be an attractive option for people who own a home. Most lenders will suggest borrowing money against your home equity. The equity is the difference between current selling value of your home and the amount of money you owe on it. Lenders let you take the loan on the 80% value of home equity. Never borrow more than the equity. If you do so, you are taking more than the home worth. It is simply a disaster because if you have to sell your home, you won't be able to do so since you owe more than the worth. Putting your home at risk can be an emotional experience for many. Let's not be emotional. We need to make a wise decision. There are some things to consider:

· If you haven't yet paid the home loan, you'll have to pay both loans if the bank sells your home.

· If you lose your job or you become sick, you can easily fall back to pay the home equity loan.

There are also some advantages of getting the home equity loan. The interest rate is usually lower. If you borrow less than 100,000$, the interest rate becomes tax deductible. 100,000$ is a big amount, and I recommend getting a smaller amount if possible. A minor amount is easy to pay, and you do not take many risks. Every debt paying option comes with some risks. Analyze your personal situation and make decisions wisely.

According to the Federal Truth, in Lending Act, you have three days to cancel the loan in writing. If you do so, the lender must cancel the lien on your home.

Borrowing against your life insurance policy

This can be a great option if you have a complete life insurance policy. You can easily borrow against the life insurance policy. Each year you'll have to pay a cash amount. You'll also earn an interest rate value as the policy's cash. Now, this trick has many advantages except a great disadvantage. If you die, the insurance policy deducts the remaining loan amount from the policy's proceedings. Your family may ending up having less than they expected. Overall, you get two benefits from this option:

. No credit check and no application filling.

. You do not have to repay the money after borrowing.

Make sure to read all the company policies and ask about any hidden fees or costs involved.

Borrowing from your retirement plan

This may seem like another attractive idea, but do not be a victim of it. Let's read why. If you are an employee, you have been enrolled in a retirement plan sponsored by your employer. The amount in your retirement account is treated as tax-deferred income. You do not pay taxes until you start withdrawing money after retirement. After retirement, each withdrawal is considered your income and hence it becomes eligible for tax calculation. The retirement plans allow you to withdraw 50,000$ or 50% of the total amount. If you have 120,000$ in the account, you can withdraw 50,000$. If the total amount is 20,000$, you can only get 10,000$ with the condition that you must pay back every penny within five years. An interest rate is also applied to the borrowed money. All is good since you are borrowing your money, but you do not know what the interest rate can do for you.

Let's try to understand the scenario.

. If you do not pay the amount back in 5 years, you will pay a 10% fine on the unpaid amount. The unpaid amount is considered as an early withdrawal from your retirement account, and you'll be taxed on the account. Look for supplementary pages when your next tax documents arrive at your doorstep.

. Unlike other options, there is no one pressurizing you to repay the money. A vast majority of people borrow money, but procrastination never lets them pay the actual amount.

. If you become sick or you lose your job, how are you planning to repay the amount while maintaining your life standard?

. Your golden years are going to be blank if you do not deposit money back in the account.

. If you lose the job for whatever reason (Your boss fired you or find a better job), the employer will force you to pay every penny within a very short time i.e. 30 days-90 days. Most likely, you cannot pay the dues. Since the amount is an early withdrawal, it will regularly be taxed in addition to the 10% penalty.

Hardship Withdrawal

Financially speaking, the withdrawal is different from taking a loan. A loan is returnable. You take some funds out of the retirement account, and you are eligible to pay back that money. If you become eligible for a hardship withdrawal, you cannot repay that money. To be eligible, you must show that you seriously need money, and you cannot rely on any other source. Your employer will determine whether you need an emergency or not. If qualified, you will have to pay federal taxes and a 10% penalty on the withdrawal.

Here is a quick overview of what we have discussed so far. The fear of future can hurt your judgment and thinking ability. These tips will help you stay on the track.

. Never accept debt consolidation from debt consolidation firms. These firms promise to lend you money to pay the debt. The interest rate is usually much higher, and you have to risk your home.

. Taking finance company loan is another dangerous option. Not only, but the loan also comes with increased interest rate; it damages the credit history.

. Beware of lenders who promise to give a huge amount without any upfront payment. That may seem like an attractive option, but it is a terrible way. Those lenders will not only charge penalties, but you may risk valuable assets.

. I checked advertisements and was shocked to see companies negotiating for you to get debt consolidation. Those companies ask you to send monthly payments. They use that to pay your debt. The reality is that these companies never pay your debt. These efforts just impact your credit history negatively while the debt interest rate increases.

If the need to negotiate arises, you can do it yourself. Contact all the creditors at an early stage. When the matter starts getting out of control, sit with creditors and see if they can help you. With negotiation, you can reduce the debt amount, or you can work out some ways to pay it quickly. You do not receive positive answers every time, but at least you can try to get a success rate of 50%. A little help can save you from bankruptcy. It gives you confidence and a plan to go in the right direction.

Our society places a tremendous value on material possessions. We may talk about equality and rights of human beings, but human beings lose respect, value, and self-worth when they owe money to the creditors. Something happens to your soul; it feels like things can never be right, or you cannot make the right decision. Take a deep breath. Clear your mind of all negative thoughts.

How to find a reputable finance consulting agency?

In difficult times, you must consult a reputable finance consulting agency. How to find a trustworthy finance consultant?

The agency helps you develop a budget. It reviews your financial situation. Suggestions are made for cutting expenses. You get tips to earn more and good advice to take control of debts.

. The agency assesses your financial situation.

. The agency creates a plan to manage the debts. It devises methods for you to generate smooth cash flow. It may suggest a debt management program or any other method to pay the debt. Agency will also guide you how you can get the loan? What are the best options and the best interest rate? Mostly, credit counseling agencies help you with unsecured loans.

. Consultation provides you with good advice. After all, the good financial education is what you need to make wise decisions.

Here are some tips to work with reputable credit counseling firms:

. Check if they are federally approved, non-profit, tax-exempt credit counseling agency?

. Ask if they are a licensed agency?

. Get a list of their services.

. Ask for their charges.

. Ask about their credit counselors. Check their background, salary, and license.

. Get a written contract if you decide to work with the agency.

Chapter 18: Stay Focused Even With Emergencies

With budgets, the more consistent you are, the more growth and change you will see. The word 'consistent' can be intimidating. It comes close to the word 'perfection' making it a daunting word. But this is because people confuse consistency with inflexibility. I will illustrate the difference with an example.

Let's say you want to learn how to play an electric guitar. You commit to practicing an hour a day, six days a week. That sounds like a reasonable goal, but what if you underestimated how busy you will be next semester? You might find that you can no longer practice an hour a day. Consistency does not mean practicing an hour every day when you are clearly overstretched, that is inflexibility. Inflexibility is unreasonable, straining, and breaking. Consistency means practicing every day, even if that is 30 minutes a day or less. The "every day" is what is important. When you suddenly find yourself with more time, you can go back to an hour a day or more. Budgets are like that, your circumstances will change, and you will have to adjust. Unexpected expenses and situations can come up. You can find yourself having to move, or your income might decrease. Whatever the circumstances, you need to be able to evaluate your situation and adjust accordingly from time to time.

This consistency is what will help you when you hit emergencies down the road. What's even better is an emergency fund to help with emergencies. Having a savings account in conjunction with an emergency fund can help carry you through difficult times. There are many ways to set up an emergency fund. They all entail putting some of your money in your original budget towards your emergency fund. I suggest taking half of what is in your budget and allocating it to the emergency fund. So if you are saving and investing 30% of your earnings, you can send half of that to your emergency fund. As a rule, just like your savings account, your emergency fund should have its own account separate from your checking account. This separation protects you from yourself. When they are within the same account, there is a danger of you spending the money. This can happen by mistake or intentionally. The separation you create in your account creates an extra step. That extra step may be the time your conscience needs to convince you otherwise.

You need to treat your emergency funds like a bill or an immovable expense. Psychologically you need to convince yourself that it is. Think of it like an insurance that you are selling to yourself for circumstances that you cannot predict. It will motivate you. An emergency fund will give you a reassuring, happy feeling. You will know you are prepared for any unexpected circumstances that may arise.

It will make you feel in control, successful, and confident in yourself and your life's capacity to move forward.

When do you know if you have saved enough? Experts say you have to save an amount that can cover your living expenses for three to six months. This is based on the assumption that this is ample time to recover from an emergency. But this will differ for everybody, there is no limit, but three to six months is a good place to start. I advise celebrating each milestone; for instance, if you save enough to survive a month, celebrate it because it is also significant—every little victory counts.

Emergency funds can help with a wide range of situations. It can help with repairs and other costs that come with owning things, whether the thing you own is a home, a computer, or home appliances. Repair and maintenance costs are often unpredictable, coming at a time when we are not prepared. Emergency funds can help with debt during times of financial stress. So if you lose your job or get temporarily laid off, you can dip into your emergency fund to keep up your debt payments. In a gig economy, it can be hard to have a stable cash flow, this means some months you might find yourself with less money and some months you might find yourself with more. Clients come and go. To help you stay afloat, a budget and emergency fund can help you when gigs are scarce. An emergency fund casts itself as versatile insurance.

Chapter 19: Start Creating Your Budget

Know your spending history

In creating a budget plan, the first step is to track your spending history. You need to know how much money you spend every month. Start collecting your bills, receipts, and credit card statements in order to have an accurate estimation of your monthly expenses. Sum up all your expenses and revenues for the past few months to know your total expenses. By doing this, you will be able to know how to design your budget plan that will fit in your financial status.

Also, identify how you're spending money currently.

Choosing a budgeting material

Nowadays, there are a lot of personal finance software that can be used to help you budget. These programs have many features that help you design your budget, understand your spending habits, and help you project cash flow in the future. Some of the examples of these budgeting software are Microsoft money, BudgetPulse, AceMoney, Quicken and Mint.

If you choose not to use budgeting software, you can still design your own budget plan in a spreadsheet. You can choose Microsoft excel or you can download a free spreadsheet program as long as it is compatible with your computer. Using a spreadsheet in tracking your income and expenses will help you minimize mistakes and make calculations easier. It can keep a running total of your finances which automatically adjusts every time you enter a new expense data.

If you want a least-expensive option that doesn't require a computer or an additional software expense, you can choose to use a notebook to record your budget plan. However, using a notebook is quite dangerous because you might misplace it and pages can be tore or get wet. It's also difficult to track and record long-term expenses with a notebook.

Calculate your income

Make a list of your income sources such as self-employment income, wages, pensions, commissions, child maintenance, or other regular sources of income. If you are a freelancer or an independent contractor, estimate how much you're likely to earn in a month. Calculate your income and subtract your estimated taxes to arrive at a more accurate amount of money left.

If you are a regular and salaried employee, subtract automatically your monthly taxes.

Make a list of your expenditures

The next step is to make a list of all your monthly expenses. This includes the bills that you have to pay every month, the amount of money that you spend on groceries, transportation costs, utility bills, or the amount of money that goes to shopping and other stuff. It will help you have an accurate view of your spending habits and unnecessary expenses. Gather all your credit card statements, receipts, bills, or other spending information to have an exact record of your spending.

Identifying expenses is an important process because it will help you know your common mistakes in spending and helps you track unnecessary expenses. The main purpose of it is to find out where your money goes every month.

Start recording your expenses from the least to the bigger amounts. You can also categorize your expenses into fixed and optional. Fixed expenses include bills, food, loan debts, transportation expenses, and other necessary things such as household products and clothing. While optional expenses include entertainment, luxuries, vacation funds, and savings.

Set priorities

One of the most important processes in creating your budget is separating your needs from wants. In designing a budget, you should know how to set your priorities. As you track your spending, you will discover that some of your money is spent on things that you don't really need. When you don't make a clear list of the things that you need, you will most likely purchase things that you may not need or spend more than you've planned. You should cut back on impulse spending when you're starting on a budget.

The key to having an effective budget is to separate your needs from wants or setting a priority list. Know the things that you really need and make them your priorities. If you don't know how to distinguish your needs from wants, try not having some random things for a period of time. If you realize that you cannot really live without it, then it is a need.

Set your goals

After you have made a clear monitor about your finances, you are now able to determine how much money you have left every month. Decide what to do with that money and set goals to accomplish.

In setting your goals, you need to identify what is important to you. Write down the things you want to have or a financial status that you want to achieve. By doing it, you will have a strong motivation in maintaining your designed budget.

You can have short-term goals such as:

- Having a house for the family

- Help your family members attain an education

- Start a business

- Pay off credit cards

- Apply for a business loan

- Buy a new car

- Travel or have a vacation

- Buy a new appliance

While on the other hand, long-term goals may include retirement plans, help children start out on their own or live without financial worries. You can choose whatever is important to you and design your goals well. Most people overspend because they don't clearly know what they want to do with their money. That is why they often use it to buy unnecessary things and spend money randomly. Clear goals will help you build your plan and serve as targets to aim. By having it, you can easily map out how you will achieve them.

After setting your goals, plan how much you need to save every month and for how long are you going to do it. Think also of how to accomplish that savings. Your goals should be realistic. Start planning for your success!

Start designing your budget plan

After you have ensured that your expenses do not exceed your income, set your goals and have separated your needs from wants, you are now ready to design your budget. This is where you make a plan based on what you've learned from your spending information.

Organize your budget plan into categories such as incomes, necessary expenses, bills, and other expenditures depending on your situation. Calculate your expenses and make some adjustments in a way that you will still have enough money to save. Make a list of the things that you need to buy every month and calculate your bills in order to estimate the amount of money that will come out of your income. Make sure that your expenses are lesser than your income. Think of different ways on how to save money every month.

Design your budget in a way that you can easily understand and monitor your finances. You can also ask your friends for ideas on a budget plan, try different designs, and find which one fits you.

Chapter 20: What Are The Elements Of A Small-Business Budget?

What makes a decent spending plan?

The best spending plans are straightforward and adaptable. In the event that conditions change (as they do), your spending limit can flex to give you a reasonable image of where you remain consistently. The budgeting technique involves the use of sheer planning cooperated with efficient role of coordination. To do a simple budgeting, one has to follow the subsequent components to attain a better budget of it.

Each great spending plan ought to incorporate seven parts:

1. Your evaluated income

This is the sum you hope to make from the closeout of products or administrations. It's the money you acquire the entryway paying little respect to what you spent to arrive. This is the main line on your financial limit. It very well may be founded on a year ago's numbers, or dependent on industry midpoints in case you're a startup.

2. Your fixed expenses

These are on the whole your normal, reliable costs that don't change as indicated by the amount you make— things like lease, protection, utilities, bank charges, bookkeeping and legitimate administrations, and gear renting.

Further perusing: Fixed Costs (Everything You Need to Know)

3. Your variable expenses

These change as indicated by creation or deals volume, and are firmly identified with "expenses of products sold", for example anything identified with the generation or acquisition of the item your business sells. This may incorporate crude materials, stock, creation costs, bundling, or transporting. Other variable expenses can incorporate deals commission, Visa charges, and travel. An unmistakable spending plan traces what you hope to spend on every one of these expenses.

The expense of pay rates can fall under both fixed and variable expenses. For instance, your center in-house group is typically connected with fixed expenses, while creation or assembling groups— anything identified with generation of products—are treated as factor costs. Ensure you record your diverse compensation costs in the right territory of your spending limit.

4. Your irregular expenses

One-off costs fall outside the standard work your business does. These are startup costs like moving workplaces, hardware, furniture, and programming, just as different costs identified with dispatch and research.

5. Your income

This is all the cash going into and out of a business. You have positive income if there is more cash coming into your business than going out, over a set timeframe. This is most effectively determined by subtracting the measure of cash accessible toward the start of a set timeframe and toward the end.

Since income is the oxygen of each business, ensure you screen this week by week, or possibly month to month. You could be rounding it up, however not have enough cash available to pay your providers.

6. Your benefit

Benefit is the thing that you bring home after the entirety of your costs are deducted from your income. Developing benefits mean a developing business. Here you'll design out how much benefit you intend to make, in view of your anticipated income, costs, and cost of products sold. On the off chance that the distinction among income and costs (otherwise known as "overall revenues") aren't the place you'd like them to be, you have to reconsider your expense of products sold, and think about raising costs. Or then again on the off chance that you figure you can't crush any more net revenue out of your business, consider boosting the Advertising and Promotions line in your spending limit to expand all out deals.

7. A spending adding machine

This is a useful instrument to see precisely where you stand with regards to your business spending arranging. It may sound self-evident, however getting every one of the numbers in your financial limit in one simple to-peruse rundown is extremely useful.

In your spreadsheet, make an outline page with a column for every one of the spending classes above. This is the structure of your fundamental spending plan. At that point by every classification, list the aggregate sum you've planned. Make another section to one side—when the timeframe closes, use it to list the real sums spent in every class. This gives you a preview of your spending that is anything but difficult to discover without jumping into layers of swarmed spreadsheets.

Each fall, the CPAs and business counselors at Doeren Mayhew urge our customers to direct three significant arranging ventures for the new year – charge arranging, creating or overhauling your vital arrangement and building up a business spending plan. Considering that, here are six key segments of a business spending plan:

A portrayal of your business and its market. You may think you have a sound spending plan for your organization, however it won't be exact if it's for your organization three years prior. Make a concise portrayal out of absolutely what you're doing well now, how your market is going (hot? cold?), and what monetary variables might be influencing how your cash is planned.

Clarification of how the spending bolsters the organization's crucial, qualities, objectives and targets. To be remembered for the spending limit, things should integrate with and bolster generally speaking organization objectives. In the event that you can't successfully exhibit how a thing empowers a specific objective, you should scrutinize its legitimacy. In the event that you don't as of now have a statement of purpose, make one to assist you with this part.

Detail subtleties for allotting reserves. Run of the mill models incorporate staffing, land, hardware and material needs. In spite of the fact that it tends to be dull to keep up a nitty gritty spending plan for all organization uses, it's great income the board. Your financial limit can encourage cost following and help control going through choices to line up with your business objectives.

Desires for estimating execution against the financial limit. For examination purposes, a financial limit is valuable in particular on the off chance that you update it normally so it precisely reflects genuine spending. For example, you may have underbudgeted or overbudgeted on certain things and, in this way, spent pretty much than you foreseen.

Supporting supplements. These may incorporate a chronicled spending plan and results investigation. Additionally consider connecting synopsis archives for every division, tables and diagrams delineating business sector and cost patterns, hierarchical graphs and a glossary of terms.

An official outline. This can be a decent method to concentrate the entirety of the data in your financial limit and furnish you with some commonsense "takeaways." More significant, an official outline can make your spending progressively edible to loan specialists and outside speculators.

Improve your odds of development by covering these bases in your arrangement.

Numerous private ventures do not have a full money related arrangement.

Proof shows that total money related plans are basic to the long haul achievement and development of your business: A Palo Alto Software study found that business people with finished marketable strategies were more than twice as prone to effectively develop their business as the individuals who had no arrangement or a deficient monetary arrangement. Here's a manual for the six key components of an effective independent company budgetary arrangement. You can discover layouts for these monetary arrangement segments by means of the SBA or SCORE.

1. Deals estimating

You ought to have a gauge of your business income for consistently, quarter and year. Distinguishing any examples in your business cycles will assist you with bettering comprehend your business just as plan out advertising activities and development techniques. An occasional business can mean to improve deals in the previous offseason to turn into an all year adventure, while another business may turn out to be better arranged by understanding connection in upticks and downturns in business because of variables, for example, the climate or economy.

Deals gauging is likewise the establishment for defining organization development objectives. For example, expect to improve your business 10 percent over each past period.

2. Cost expense

A full cost arrangement incorporates customary costs, anticipated future costs and related costs.

Standard costs are the current progressing expenses of your business, including operational costs like lease, utilities and finance. Ordinary costs identify with standard business exercises that happen every year, for example, gathering participation, publicizing and promoting spend, or the workplace Christmas party. A full rundown of normal costs will make it simpler to recognize basic costs from costs that can be decreased or dispensed with if necessary.

Expected future costs are known future costs, for example, charge rate increments, expanded the lowest pay permitted by law or upkeep needs. By and large, spending plan ought to likewise be dispensed for surprising future costs, for example, storm harm. Making arrangements for future costs will assist you with guaranteeing your business is monetarily arranged by means of spending decrease, increments in deals or budgetary help.

Related costs are the evaluated expenses of different activities, for example, the expense to obtain and prepare another contract, open another store, or grow conveyance to another domain. An exact gauge of related costs will help you appropriately deal with your development and prevent you from surpassing your cost capacities. Similarly as with anticipated future costs, seeing how much capital is required to achieve different development objectives will assist you with settling on the correct choice about financing alternatives.

3. Proclamation of money related position (resources and liabilities)

Resources and liabilities are the establishment of your business' monetary record and the essential determinants of your total assets. Following both will guarantee you are expanding your business' latent capacity esteem. Independent ventures much of the time underestimate their benefits, for example, apparatus, property or stock, and neglect to appropriately represent extraordinary bills.

Your monetary record, or budgetary position, offers a more complete perspective on your business' wellbeing than a benefit and misfortune explanation or an income report. A benefit and misfortune articulation shows how the business performed over a particular timespan, while a monetary record shows the budgetary situation of the business on some random day.

4. Income projection

Like anticipating your costs, a shrewd entrepreneur ought to have the option to foresee their income on a month to month, quarterly and yearly premise. Anticipating income for the entire year enables you to stretch out beyond any money related battles or difficulties. It can likewise assist you with recognizing an income issue before it contrarily impacts your business.You can set the most proper installment terms, for example, the amount you charge forthright or how long in the wake of invoicing you anticipate installment.

An income projection gives you a reasonable take a gander at what cash will be left toward the finish of every month, empowering you to design conceivable extension or different ventures. It additionally empowers unrivaled planning, for example, going through less one month for the foreseen money needs of another.

5. Equal the initial investment examination

This area breaks down fixed costs comparative with the benefit earned by each extra unit you produce and sell. This is fundamental to understanding your business' income and potential expenses versus benefits of development or development of your yield. Having your costs completely fleshed out, as portrayed above, will make your make back the initial investment examination increasingly precise and helpful.

Make back the initial investment examination is additionally the most ideal approach to decide your valuing. The fitting cost for your items and administrations can improve benefit quicker than expanding yield. A make back the initial investment investigation can disclose to you what number of units you'd have to sell at different value focuses to take care of your expenses. You should expect to set a value that gives you an agreeable edge over your costs while staying aggressive.

6. Tasks plan

To maintain your business as effectively as could reasonably be expected, create a nitty gritty outline of your operational needs. Understanding what jobs are required to work your business at different volumes of yield, how much yield or work every worker can deal with, and the expenses of each phase of your inventory network will enable you to settle on educated choices for your business' development and effectiveness.

It's imperative to firmly control costs, for example, finance or inventory network, comparative with development. An activities plan will likewise make it simpler to decide whether there is space to enhance your tasks or production network by means of mechanization, new innovation or predominant store network merchants.

Chapter 21: Ask This Question And Be Less Stressed

You have read from a previous chapter about the difference between wants and needs. Your 'wants' are the things that you would like to have, perhaps to make yourself more presentable, more comfortable or more appealing to society. Expensive jewelry and accessories, trendy clothes, branded shoes, and high-tech gadgets mostly belong to the 'wants' category. You can live without them, but your life will seem better when you have them.

When you wear the latest trends in clothes, accessories and shoes, people will consider you a fashion icon and will want to hang out with you. If you have the latest smartphone, you can download more apps and connect with more people on social media, uploading photos and videos that you took using your new, expensive gadget. On the other hand, if you wear basic and plain clothes, people will hardly notice you. You can pass by them and they will not give you a second look. If your phone is old and does not have a lot of features, you will not have much chance to sit at the 'cool table' with all the 'cool people' and their 'cool stuff'.

Your 'needs' are the things that you really need to have to survive and live normally in this world. You need food and water, and a roof over your head and clothing to protect your body. You also need electricity to help you accomplish tasks easier and faster, such as cooking, doing laundry, etc. You need personal care products, such as soap, shampoo, and toothpaste to help you maintain good hygiene. You also need to have insurance to keep you and your family protected in case of unexpected circumstances.

Now that you have a clear idea on what 'wants' and 'needs' are, you should always think twice before spending your money on anything. If you see something that you like, ask yourself if you really want it and

not if you can afford it. Say, you found a really nice sweater at a boutique and it's on sale. You can afford it, but would you buy it?
Before reaching for your wallet, think carefully what impact that sweater has on you. Do you really want it because you need it or you just want to add to your wardrobe? If your reason is the latter, then you are better off not buying that sweater even if it's on sale. However, if the weather is cold and your old sweater no longer fits you or has a huge hole in it, then you can go ahead and purchase the sweater.

Apply the same theory in other aspects of your life. Before you pay for something, be sure to think thoroughly.

Chapter 22: Getting Help With Budgeting

Budgeting is hard for just about everyone, so there's no shame in seeking out some extra help. In this chapter, we'll go over all your options, such as talking to a professional, taking classes, and making use of online and app-based programs. Whether you are new to budgeting, want to explore another style, or something big happened that requires you change things up, there's someone or some service out there that can make the process much easier.

Professionals

You have several options when it comes to professionals who can help. It depends on what your goals are. Financial planners, debt counselors, and others should be considered.

Financial adviser vs. financial planner

"Financial adviser" is an umbrella term that refers to anyone who gets paid to provide financial advice. They can specialize in different areas, like estate planning, tax planning, debt repayment, and more. Depending on their area of expertise, they'll have different licenses and certifications that qualify them. As an example, if they help clients manage investments or trade stocks, they usually have to have a Series 65 securities license.

A financial planner's job is to look at your financial situation, make suggestions, and perform certain actions, like investing money for you. They are a type of financial advisor, and often specialize in a certain area, like retirement planning or saving for college. Their goal is to help you create a plan to meet your long-term goals. They will either be a certified financial planner (CFP) or chartered financial consultant (ChFC).

Should you seek out a financial adviser or a financial planner? It doesn't really matter what a person calls themselves.

You want to look at their credentials. Let's assume you aren't super wealthy and just want someone to help you budget for long-term goals. Find a CFP. These planners have completed education and passed an exam to get that title. They are also required to have three years of full-time experience and maintain good standing with a Board's code of ethics and conduct. This means they have to give you good advice that benefits you.

How do I pay for a financial planner?

Financial planners are paid using one of three methods: fee-only, fee-based, and commission-based. A fee-only planner is paid a flat hourly rate, as well as a percentage of the total assets (usually 1-2%) they manage for their clients. That means they only get paid a lot of money if you're worth a lot of money. They are not allowed to try and sell you anything, like life insurance.

Fee-based planners get a fee and usually a commission on an investment they sell you. This could encourage the planner to try and sell an expensive investment, because they would get more of the commission. A commission-based planner is only paid by companies in exchange for the planner selling their products, so they can be very biased. If you're concerned about getting ripped off by someone without integrity, go with a fee-only planner.

Debt counselor vs. credit counselor

If you need to pay down debts and you're struggling, a debt counselor or credit counselor are the best options. What's the difference?

A debt counselor deals with debt settlement, which means they arrange your debt settlements with creditors or collectors in exchange for a fee. How it works: you contact a debt settlement company or a debt settlement lawyer. They contact your creditors and negotiate settlements. In the meanwhile, you make monthly payments to the debt settlement company, which they put in account for your creditors. They will also use this account for their own fees. Before they take a fee, however, they must reach a successful conclusion with your creditors that's different than the agreement that stood before you came to the debt settlement company. Also, you must have made at least one payment to the creditor based on that new agreement. This protects you from debt companies asking for a fee right away before they've settled anything. You want to be sure the debt counselor you choose is reliable; it isn't unheard of for a settlement company to close, taking all your money with them, leaving your creditors knocking on your door.

What about a credit counselor? These professionals offer advice on how to pay down your debts and become debt-free. They will need access to your income, expenses, debts, and so on in order to get the clearest picture possible of your financial health. Once they have all that information, they can offer advice on what to do. They might suggest a debt settlement lawyer or company. Credit counselors usually offer very affordable services, because they understand you're struggling financially if you're looking for help with debt. Many credit counselors are part of nonprofits that don't charge anything. The National Foundation for Credit Counseling is one of these non-profits, and they also offer financial education programs. 32 out of the United States' 50 states require a license to practice credit counseling, so if you live in one of the states that doesn't require a specific certification, be cautious. Many credit counselors are also licensed financial planners, so that's a good place to start.

Education resources

Whether you choose to go with a financial planner or other professional, you probably want to educate yourself a bit more on finances and good budgeting. You're reading this book, so you're clearly already taking the initiative. There are endless options for further education, many of which are very affordable or free. Some will cost money, but you often get the best advice. Start out with what's free, though.

Books

Books are a great way to start learning about budgeting. You don't even have to buy them; get them from your library. Most library systems will at least have a few of these:

Broke Millennial by Erin Lowry

Great for people just learning to budget, even if you aren't a millennial. Topics include budgets, salary negotiations, being transparent with your partner about money, and of course, student debt. Lowry also has a Broke Millennial book for beginner investors.

The Everything Budgeting Book by Tere Stouffer

A comprehensive step-by-step guide on creating the perfect budget. There are chapters on figuring out your financial health, how to reduce budget expenses, getting through unemployment, and so much more.

I Will Teach You To Be Rich by Ramit Sethi

This book distills complex financial issues into very simple language, and makes following his tips very simple as well. If you're not much of a reader and don't like dense books, this is a great one to start with.

Total Money Makeover by Dave Ramsey

If you haven't heard of Dave Ramsey yet, that will definitely change as you get more into budgeting. He's considered the top dog in his field, and this book is one of the best.

Your Money Or Your Life by Vicki Robin and Joe Dominguez

If the fixation on financial wealth that often infuses the personal finance world isn't your style, this is a great palate cleanser. It focuses on how to align your personal values with your budget instead of how to get richer. It's broken down into nine steps. The book has been around for over twenty years, though it was revised and updated in 2018.

Websites

Don't want to sit down with a book? There are lots of websites dedicated to personal finance packed with useful information. Here are a few to consider:

WiseBread - This site has sections dedicated to frugal living, life hacks, career, and credit cards. You can search for specific topics of interest to see if the site has covered it. As an example, a search for "student loans" brought up a bunch of articles on topics like getting a home loan when you have student loans, how student loan interest works, and a list of companies that help pay off loans.

BankRate - This site actually began as a newsletter before the Internet, and has continued to maintain a stellar reputation. It gives information on anything bank-related, like credit cards, mortgages, and bank rates, though it also offers lots of other personal finance advice. Another cool thing about it: it hosts a wide variety of calculators for stuff like mortgages, credit cards, net worth, and more.

DailyWorth - Though it's designed specifically with women in mind, this site has useful info for everyone. You can sign up for daily emails that cover topics on how to budget, earn, save, and invest. The site is divided into sections for work, life, family, money, and retirement. When you click on an article from the site, it redirects to a HerMoney url, but it's the same site; HerMoney owns and operates DailyWorth.

Classes

There are countless online courses on finances you can find online, many for free. Udemy has a wealth of classes like

"Making Sense of Your Personal Finances," which is free, as well as paid classes like "Personal Finance: Complete Guide to Budgeting." Other platforms with classes include Coursera, FutureLearn, and SkillShare. Like the structure and access to a teacher offered by a more traditional class? There are probably financial courses offered at a community college near you. You'll need to have the time to attend and do the homework, but the benefit is you get to interact with real people and an instructor.

Best online budget tools

If you don't want to pay for the assistance of a financial coach, but you still need some guidance, an online budgeting tool is a fantastic method. These types of software can help you track spending, pay down debt, schedule payments, and so much more. Here are five that people love:

Pocketsmith

This cloud-based software lets you connect all your accounts - bank and investment - as well as loans and credit cards, so you can find out your net worth and get an accurate understanding of your financial health. You can't pay your bills, but you can schedule reminders using the calendar so you never miss a payment. You can also create daily, weekly, or monthly budgets; run "what-if" scenarios; and run projections to see what your bank account might look like in twenty years. The free Basic plan gets you 12 budgets, 2 accounts, and up to six months of forecasting. The Premium forecasts up to 10 years, gives you unlimited budgets, and more. It costs $9.95 a month or $7.50 if you pay for a year. The Super plan gives you forecasts of thirty years and all of Pocketsmith's features for $19.95 a month or $14.16 monthly for the annual plan.

Buxfer

Designed for young budgeters in their 20's, this online tool lets you forecast earnings and savings interest; tag expenses (like groceries) and set limits on them; upload financial statements; and track shared expenses, so you never owe a friend money and can keep track of any money you're owed. You can send friends money through Buxfer, too. The tagging system might take some getting used to, but once it's all set up, it's pretty useful. You can give expenses multiple tags, too, which would be tricky to track in a more traditional line-item budget. Buxfer sends you notifications if you exceed the limit of a tag category, so you can avoid overspending.

Buxfer also lets you track and manage investments and forecast your finances. To protect your data, the site is very secure with high-grade encryption and daily scans from security firms. They have five plan options, including a free one, which gives you unlimited transactions, five accounts, shared expense tracking, and more. The most expensive plan - Prime - costs $9.99 a month.

Budget Ease

If you want to use the cash-only/envelope style of budgeting, but don't want to bother with physical cash envelopes, Budget Ease brings that method into the digital world. You create a budget and "envelopes," which you label with the amount of money you want to spend for that envelope's category. For the envelopes that are for bills, you can set up reminders, so you're never late. To update the envelopes, text the amount you spent, or update the number manually on the site. To see how much you have left, set up daily or weekly alerts. Budget Ease can also project what your savings will be up to a year in the future, lets you use a credit card if necessary, and lets you upload and organize receipts.

SavvyMoney

If you need to get rid of debt as quickly as possible while building up your savings, the SavvyMoney site is a great option. You start off by entering your personal debt and banking info to the site, which calculates everything and gives you a clearer look at your situation. It also provides you with the smallest monthly payment you need to make and how long it will take to be debt-free. Next, you can take advantage of the SmartPay Plan and choose one of three debt-payment plans: debt stacking, snowball, or custom. SavvyMoney isn't free, though, you do have to pay around $15 a month, so think about if it's worth it. With that fee, you do get lots of information on money management and how to negotiate for a lower interest rate on debts.

Budget Tracker

Not really into technology? Budget Tracker is relatively simple, so even if you're wary of online tools, it's easy for most people. It's also free. It lets you create basic budgets and provides calculators for student loans, credit card debt payoff, and more, so you can figure out your financial situation and set goals. It also has features for tax deductions and kids' budgeting, so your young ones can learn good money management. If you're a small business, you can use this software for those needs, as well. The website is very basic or even outdated, according to some. It seems relatively straightforward in terms of navigation, however, and like we said, it's free.

Best apps for budgeting

If you like a really modern, clean design and want to budget right on your phone, you'll want to get an app. Many of these apps also have an online component, but let's assume you just want to use to use it on your phone or tablet. Which ones do people like the most?

Mint

Arguably the most famous budgeting app, Mint is owned by the same company that makes TurboTax and Quickbooks. There's a wealth of features, like tax reporting, bill management, investment monitoring, and more. Creating a budget is pretty easy, and you can set up alerts for late fees, overspending, rate changes, and so on. It will also automatically categorize transactions from linked accounts. To start, you have to link all your financial accounts. If this makes you nervous, know that Mint is very secure, but that might still worry you. Mint downloads months of data, so it takes a while at first, but once it's set up, updates are quick. You'll then get access to Mint's menu, which includes an overview, bills, budgets, goals, etc.

PocketGuard

This app is best if you want to stop overspending. Like Mint, it links to all your financial accounts. Using the information on your income, bills, and goals you've established, PocketGuard generates the perfect budget for you. You can tweak it, of course, if you want. With the free basic version of the app, you can set a monthly saving goal and track bills. The premium version lets you track cash (like for tips), plan for cash bills, and records your ATM withdrawals. It costs $3.99 a month, or $34.99 for a year. The "In My Pocket" feature is an algorithm that analyzes your income and expenses, and lets you know what you have left over each day. You can also set up limits on your categories and if you get close to that limit, PocketGuard will text you an alert. Using your profile info as a guide, the app even gives you tips on how to save money through an improved credit score, rebates, and more.

You Need A Budget (YNAB)

This budget app uses the zero-based style, so every dollar you make has a job. With this app, which you can also use on your computer, you can track goals, sync to multiple devices, and read all kinds of helpful blogs and articles. It used to be based on four "rules," but with the new update, it now has three: 1) give every dollar a job 2) embrace your true expenses and 3) roll with the punches. Rule #2 basically means you have more control over your budget by using funds monthly to pay for big, less frequent expenses like insurance premiums and vacations. By always putting away a little money for these larger costs, you avoid having to suddenly spend out big chunks of money. Rule #3 means you anticipate overspending in certain categories, so you tweak your budget by moving money around to compensate. Unfortunately, there is no free version of this app after the trial, and it costs $6.99 a month.

Mvelopes

If you like the cash-only style of budgeting, this app was designed for you. Your "envelopes" are different categories, like groceries, entertainment, and so on, and you specify how much money you want in each envelope for the month. Setting Mvelopes up is easy and just four steps: sync bank accounts, type in your income, create a budget, and put money in the envelopes. You can quickly click on or search for your bank in the database Mvelopes provides, but if your bank isn't on there for some reason, you can request that Mvelope add it, and they'll get back to you in 2-4 days. Connecting your accounts means you don't have to manually enter every transaction.

According to a review, it works best if you have a regular salaried income; the app can be finicky if you're paid hourly.

You do have to pay for the app after a free 30-day trial. The cheapest plan is $4 a month. The most expensive plan costs a whopping $59 a month and give you access to customized planning, financial education, and a monthly session with a personal finance trainer from Mvelopes.

Albert

If you hate math, Albert may be the app for you. It's hands-off and perfect if you want to save more money. How does it work? You connect your financial accounts to Albert, which then analyzes your income, budget, spending, and financial health. Algorithms figure out how much you can save each month without disrupting your budget. The app then automatically transfers money (between $5-$30 two or three times a week) into Albert Savings. The funds are FDIC-insured, which means they are protected by the

Federal Deposit Insurance Corporation, up to $250,000. If you want to control how much you're saving, you can do that with Albert, as well, and just tell it to transfer a specific amount. You can withdraw your Albert savings any time, fee-free.

If you want something extra, you can pay for Albert Genius, which lets you decide how much you want to pay. They suggest $4 a month, and claim that most pay $6. If you pay less than $4, we're not sure what (if anything) changes with the app. Albert Genius lets you ask Albert's financial experts any questions at any time, like, "Where's the cheapest place in my area to buy a new car?" Also with your Genius subscription, the app will pay you $1 for every $100 you save over the course of a year. If you don't pay for Genius, Albert still rewards you with 25 cents for every $100.

Honorable app mentions:

Personal Capital (free, unless you want their advisers and wealth management service)

Goodbudget (great for couples)

Digit (utilizes an automatic savings system)

Acorns (great for easy saving)

Conclusion

By now, I really hope you can see how important it is to apply fundamental budgeting and financial management principles in your every-day life.

Nothing would mean more to me than if you take everything we've covered in this book and make it part of your life.

It's worked for me; it can work for you too.

I understand it's not easy to make these changes in your life and stick to them every day. But if you do, suddenly it won't be discipline that moves you toward financial success, but habit.

Once again, I thank you for purchasing and reading this book.

Now it's time to step into a new, prosperous future.

And Finally:

www.ingramcontent.com/pod-product-compliance
Lightning Source LLC
Chambersburg PA
CBHW071208210326
41597CB00016B/1731